STRATEGIES

Getting and Keeping the Job You Want

STRATEGIES

Getting and Keeping the Job You Want

Sharon K. Ferrett, Ph.D.
Humboldt State University

GLENCOE
McGraw-Hill

New York, New York   Columbus, Ohio   Woodland Hills, California   Peoria, Illinois

Send all inquiries to:
Glencoe/McGraw-Hill
936 Eastwind Drive
Westerville, OH 43081

Library of Congress Cataloging-in-Publication Data

Ferrett, Sharon K.
        Strategies: getting and keeping the job you want / Sharon K. Ferrett
                p.   cm.
        Includes index.
        ISBN 0-256-14229-7
        1. Job hunting.   2. Vocational guidance.   3. Success.   I. Title
        HF5382.7.F47   1966
        650.14—dc20
                                                                        95–6558

Printed in the United States of America.
        6 7 8 9 10 11 12   079   03 02 01 00 99

To the memory of my dad, Albert L. Ferrett, for teaching me to look ahead.

To my mom, Velma Hollenbeck Ferrett, for teaching me to enjoy every day.

To my husband, Sam, and my daughters, Jennifer and Sarah, for teaching me what is really important.

PREFACE

For many students, making job and career decisions can be overwhelming. When I began thinking about *Strategies: Getting and Keeping the Job You Want,* I sat down to consider how I could guide job seekers through the exciting, but often stressful, steps of the job search. As I began writing, I asked myself "What are the most important skills for getting and keeping the *right* job?"

After many discussions with colleagues and students past and present, I concluded that above all *confidence*—in oneself and in one's ability to make good decisions and sound choices—is crucial to any successful job search. Confidence, along with the concrete strategies and guidelines presented in this book, can help you:

- Plan a systematic job search that gets results.
- Assess and define your current skills in a meaningful way.
- Feel secure about networking.
- Create resumés that put your best foot forward.
- Write positive, confident cover letters.
- Feel good about interviewing.
- Keep up your morale and energy.
- Build professional rapport.
- Make the right choices, using critical thinking and problem solving.
- Keep your job and get promoted.

FOCUS ON SKILLS

The Benefit Factor

Job hunting is a specialized skill, like learning to ski, becoming a master craftsperson, or learning to cook. During your job search, you will need to learn and practice skills and techniques that lead to the best job and career opportunities. Throughout this book you'll find numerous exercises on assessing your existing skills; translating these skills into job skills; setting goals; creating interesting and accurate resumés, cover letters, and applications; honing face-to-face interview questions and answers; and writing concise and effective follow-up letters. In addition, you'll learn specific techniques for keeping your job once you have it, by staying tuned to workplace relationships, developing interpersonal skills, monitoring your own performance, and building rapport with others on the job.

FOCUS ON PROBLEM SOLVING

Problem Solving

The ability to make decisions using focused critical thinking is an essential skill both during the job-search process and on the job. Throughout this book, you will find opportunities to practice your problem solving skills. A recurrent chapter feature, "Problem Solving at Work" presents case studies that apply problem solving strategies to job-search related challenges. These include: translating personal skills into professional ones, making sound career choices, and building an effective network.

FOCUS ON TODAY'S WORKPLACE

Workplace Trends

The workplace has undergone radical changes in the recent past and promises to change further as we move into the 21st century. With the growth of technology and telecommunications, shifts in management theory and practice, and changes in the makeup of the workforce, today's workplace looks and feels very different from 5 or 10 years ago. To increase your chances of success in the job search as well as on the job, it is essential to stay informed of the trends reshaping jobs today. "Workplace Trends" boxes in every chapter focus on issues that matter to prospective employees *and* employers, including teamwork, the virtual office, adapting to change, employee empowerment, technology, training, diversity, and more.

FOCUS ON ATTITUDE

Scaling the Wall

Finding a job is a demanding process. It can be confusing, frustrating, and difficult, even in good times. In tough times, it can be daunting to say the least. It may sometimes be difficult to maintain a positive attitude in the face of discouragement. To keep your attitude positive, be sure to review "Hitting the Wall" and "Scaling the Wall" in each chapter. These features acknowledge some of the barriers common to the job search, and provide constructive suggestions for getting past them. "Knockout Factors" and "Success Factors lists" also show how to anticipate and avoid snags in the job search.

Take Charge!

As you begin your search for the right job now, and as you move into future jobs, keep in mind the following empowerment strategies.

1. Be a lifelong learner. Your education does not stop when you leave the classroom. By learning new skills throughout your life, you'll stay current with changes in developments in your field and increase your value to current and potential employers. Your only job security is learning new skills.

2. Be a problem solver. All jobs call on problem solving skills and creativity. Take the time to explore creative options when faced with a problem.

3. Use critical thinking. The best jobs go to those who can use critical thinking to make sound decisions.

4. Network. Build a strong network of contacts and supporters, both inside and beyond your field.

5. Develop personal qualities. Being dependable and reliable, keeping a positive attitude, and being an enthusiastic team player who shows honesty and integrity, are personal qualities you can refine and build.

6. Focus on the benefit factor. Employers hire you for what you can do for them. At every step of the way, be prepared to highlight what you have to offer. Once you get a job, continually ask yourself how you can add value to the company.

7. Do your homework. Develop a broad and current knowledge of your industry by staying on top of trends in the field.

8. Focus on the big picture. Be aware of major projects, competitors, goals, new products, and customer concerns of the company you work for or would like to work for.

9. Be prepared. Be ready to look for a new job at any time. Keep your resumé up to date and feel confident about putting your job-search skills to work.

10. Stay positive! Develop a resourceful, confident, and determined state of mind. Stay enthusiastic and persistent. Keep your goals in mind.

Acknowledgements

Special thanks go to the following reviewers whose comments during manuscript development were invaluable.

Elizabeth Peak-Fortun, Allen County Community College (Iola, KS); Marie Smith, Lasell College (Newton, MA); Elizabeth Zorn, Four C Business College (Waco, TX); Candyce Skimin, National Education Center (Oak Lawn, IL); Jean Rohrer, Hagerstown Business College (Hagerstown, MD); Ed Cole, Indiana Business College (Indianapolis, IN); Jane Bollman, American Institute of Commerce (Davenport, IA); Amy Zukaukis/Christopher Caresani, Pittsburgh Technical Institute (Pittsburgh, PA); Anita Brownstein, Long Island Business Institute (Commack, NY); Jean Haley, Southern Ohio College (Fairfield, OH); Susan Wolfe, Housatonic Community Technical College (Bridgeport, CT); Linda Leach, Bladen Community College (Dublin, NC); Viv Dudley, Danville Area Community College (Danville, IL)

Contents

Assessment: The First Step

Introduction

Like any change and challenge, the job-search process involves taking stock of your strengths, areas you want to improve, personal qualities, values, goals, abilities, and skills. You will learn to take an proactive role in your job search and to plan it in a systematic and organized manner. This includes using self-assessment to determine skills and abilities and mapping out a strategy for achieving your goals. Assessing your strengths and values will help you lay the foundation for building skills in networking, exploring jobs, writing your cover letter and resumé, and interviewing. You will begin to see the connection between these activities and getting and keeping the job you want.

You will learn the importance of creative problem solving and critical thinking throughout the job-search process.

—

Learning Objectives

In Chapter 1, you will learn

- The steps involved in the job-search process.

- The importance of self-assessment.

- How to compile a database.

- How to creatively solve problems.

- The importance of critical thinking in making decisions.

- How to determine your personality and team style.

1

The Job-Search Process

Seeing the big picture of the job-search process and mapping out a step-by-step guide to getting a job will make the process less mysterious and overwhelming. This clear focus is essential to taking control of your job search.

The job search process can be broken down into three major stages: preparation and planning, action, and follow-up.

Stage One: Preparation and Planning

Preparation is key during the planning stage and is the foundation of the entire job search. Preparation involves self-assessment and reflection. Once you have assessed your values, interests, strengths, abilities, and needs, you can set goals. Defining what you want in a job is the first step in getting it.

The planning stage also involves creating a database that will help you prepare your resumé, a list of networking contacts, and good answers to interview questions.

Planning involves setting up a daily schedule and monitoring your progress. It includes creating a quiet place to reflect, set goals, return calls, compose your resumé and cover letters, prepare interview questions and answers, and keep your records. You must make a commitment to work hard, keep a positive attitude, and deal with rejection or negative feedback. You must also prepare yourself to keep detailed records that will help you focus and follow up on the required tasks.

Stage Two: Action

Taking action involves actively researching jobs and possible careers. It also involves networking and making contacts and phone calls. The preparation of the first stage will help you during the action stage while you are creating a resumé and cover letter, and filling out applications. The action stage also involves conducting your interviews. This is the stage when it is important to keep busy. Inactivity is the number-one cause of failure.

Stage Three: Follow-up

Follow-up involves attending to a variety of details and is important from day one of your job search. You need to follow up on your self-assessment and preparation and make certain you are on track, have returned phone calls, updated your data system, and followed up on all leads. Following up with phone calls, writing thank-you notes, and following up on job leads can create the leading edge for successful job hunters.

Creating a Record-Keeping System

The key to getting and keeping a job is to have an organized system for collecting and keeping information about yourself and job prospects. By following an organized system, you will be a person who

- Takes time to assess skills, interests, and abilities.
- Is an organized self-starter.
- Is good at solving problems and making decisions.
- Is persistent and positive.
- Creates an active network.
- Stays active and involved.
- Is confident and competent.
- Uses proven job search tools.
- Follows up on details.

Keep your record-keeping system from the first day of your job search. Buy a loose-leaf notebook, a variety of colored pens, tape, and tabs. Divide and color code each of the eight sections. For example, blue for Section 1, red for Section 2, and so on.

Section 1: Planning

- Time log of job search activities.

Section 2: Self-Assessment

- Personal database and autobiography.
- Worksheets and exercises assessing skills, interests, personal qualities, and values.
- Worksheets and exercises assessing goals.
- Worksheets and exercises assessing work style.

Section 3: Market Information

- Job advertisements.
- Job and industry trends articles.
- Standard salaries, benefits, and job descriptions for your field of interest.

Section 4: Networking

- List of all possible contacts.
- Time log of initial and follow-up contacts.
- Up-to-date references.

Section 5: Crucial Documents

- Resumés.
- Cover letter (to be adapted as needed).
- Basic application (to use as model).

Section 6: Before the Interview

- Address, phone number, and directions to interview site.
- Correct names, spelling, and pronunciation of interviewers.
- Anticipated interview questions with brief responses.
- Your own questions.

Section 7: During the Interview

- Summary of interview, listing strengths and weaknesses.
- Record of questions and responses.

Section 8: Follow-up

- Copy of thank-you notes.
- Copy of follow-up letters.
- List of companies to contact again.
- Acceptance letters.

Problem Solving

What is Creative Problem Solving?

In this chapter, and throughout the book, you'll read about problem solving, critical thinking, and the ability to make decisions. Why are these terms so important? Because they are lifelong skills that carry over from school into the world of work. In fact, mastering these skills will help you in the job-search process itself. Creative problem solving is the ability to explore new approaches, see the problem in a new light, and resolve an issue by using a step-by-step system.

Effective problem solving is an essential job skill. In fact, many employers say that problem solving is one of the most desired qualities in employees. How are you at solving problems? With a little practice, you can draw upon your creative resources and critical thinking skills to help you solve problems, including how to find a job and make sound decisions. Creative problem solving can help you during the self-assessment stage by clarifying and exploring new approaches. Too many job searchers give up their dreams, ignore their values and interests, and take the traditional, no-risk path to finding a job. Effective problem solving involves both a creative and a systematic approach.

1. Be creative and have fun. Some people approach problem solving in a creative and playful manner. They use imagination to explore new ideas, try out fresh solutions, and break through traditional thinking. They see problems as puzzles to solve and use creativity to search for innovative approaches. As children, most of us were enthusiastic, inventive, and creative. As we grew up, however, many of us became reluctant to challenge the rules and feel overwhelmed by problems or deny that they exist. Even though problem solving is a valued job skill, there is a tendency among many people to play it safe and follow established procedures rather than explore new ideas.

Think of new ways to assess your skills and weaknesses, research, and network. Don't just adopt a standard resumé, cover letter, or personal image. Look for creative ways to clearly communicate your strengths while still creating a professional and conservative style. Don't just copy canned answers to interview questions. Develop a verbal and nonverbal image that is distinct, sincere, credible, and professional.

2. Use a logical and systematic approach. Problem solving will not be overwhelming if you break the process into steps. A logical approach to problem solving includes several steps:

a. Identify the problem.

b. Gather information.

c. Explore resources.

d. Brainstorm alternatives.

e. Look at likely consequences.

f. Identify necessary resources and tools.

g. Develop and implement an action plan.

h. Select the best alternative.

i. Make a commitment to ensure success.

j. Evaluate your decision and progress.

k. Modify your plan if necessary.

In fact, these are the same steps we'll use to solve the problems associated with the job search.

Decision Making

At each stage of the job search, you will be faced with decisions. Within each broad decision, there will be many smaller decisions and problems to solve. Problem solving and critical thinking tie in to the decision making you'll do as part of your job search. Here are some questions that you will want to explore as you go through the job-search process:

1. Do I know my career objective? Have I assessed my skills, values, strengths, interests, and abilities?

2. What information can I gather that would help me decide what jobs are available and what companies I would like to apply to?

3. What traditional or nontraditional resources can help me explore jobs and find out more about certain companies?

4. Have I explored many jobs and companies—small companies, large companies, international companies?

5. If I apply to certain companies, what would be the likely consequence? Would I be more likely to gain more responsibility in a small company? Would a large company fit my values and needs?

6. Have I created an outstanding resumé and cover letter that highlights my accomplishments? What other job-search tools would help me be more successful?

7. Have I developed an action plan and set goals and daily priorities?

8. Have I narrowed my search to jobs that most match my interests, values, skills, and background?

9. Have I made a commitment to do everything possible to ensure that my job search and decisions are successful?

10. Have I evaluated my job search? Am I meeting my goals and objectives? Am I getting interviews? Am I getting job offers?

11. How should I modify my job search in order to ensure success?

Decision making is an integral part of problem solving. In order to solve a problem, you have to make decisions. Therefore, it is important to develop the ability to assess the possible consequences of your actions and become skillful at predicting cause and effect. Critical thinking and effective decision making are becoming increasingly more important job skills.

Critical Thinking

Critical thinking is required throughout the job search to see problems clearly and to make sound decisions. In your career, it is important that you be able to assess a situation as it really is and not how you wish it were. Critical thinking is a skill that uses facts, logic, and reasoning to help you make decisions and solve problems. A critical thinker is someone who has the willingness and ability to analyze, explore, probe, question, and examine issues before a decision is made. Critical thinkers use facts and reasoning to make sound decisions and solve problems. Critical thinking, then, is a valuable job and life skill that helps us analyze, reason, question, and suspend judgment until facts are gathered and weighed.

Characteristics of a Critical Thinker:

- Able to suspend judgment.
- Willing to analyze and reason.
- Able to ask pertinent questions and examine beliefs, assumptions, and opinions against facts.
- Has knowledge and awareness of common errors in judgment.
- Uses facts and logical thinking instead of biased, illogical, or wishful thinking.

Self-Assessment: A Point of Departure

Before you even start to look for a job, it is important to decide what it is you want to do, what you like to do, and what skills and abilities you have to offer. Self-knowledge is understanding your skills, strengths, capabilities, feelings, character, and motivations. It means you have done some serious reflection about what is important to you and what values you want to live your life by. It is very hard to make career decisions unless you really know yourself.

How Do I Get Started?

The planning process focuses on the following questions:

- What are my skills, values, and abilities?
- What do I want to do?
- What is out there? What job best matches my skills?
- What tools can help me best market myself?

Know Yourself

"Know thyself," Socrates advised, and indeed self-assessment is the foundation for the job hunting process. The more you know about yourself, your skills, values, attitude, and the type of work you like best, the easier it will be to market your skills. It is indeed the fortunate person who loves what she or he does and gets paid to do it. Your entire job search will be faster and smoother if you

- Identify your most marketable skills.
- Assess your strengths and weaknesses.
- Review your interests.
- Assess your values and life purpose.
- Assess your self-esteem and attitude.
- Identify creative ways you solve problems.
- Identify ways to use critical thinking in making decisions.
- Determine your goals.

The following exercise will look for patterns in how you make decisions and solve problems. It will also indicate your interests as you outline and write about your early life, school experience, sports, activities, jobs, community involvement, and how you developed skills. Let's start by reviewing your life.

Write down the important points in your life, starting with your early life. Think of your life as a series of stepping stones of major turning points, growth experiences, and events that shaped you into the person you are today. When you begin to connect these stepping stones, they present a pattern that leads you to your true preferences, abilities, and interests. The following list displays areas that you will want to explore as you write your autobiography. Which areas helped you develop a sense of worth and competency? What situations helped you creatively solve problems and use critical thinking to make sound decisions? You will discover values, accomplishments, strengths, and weaknesses. This exercise will also help when you are asked the typical interview question, "Tell me about yourself." Include the following:

- Interests, hobbies, challenges, and lessons that you learned.
- Jobs in which you learned responsibility and earned money.
- Events that point out strengths and weaknesses.
- Volunteer work and community service.
- Internships.
- Sports, special activities, or clubs.
- Achievements and awards.
- Challenges, setbacks, and disappointments.
- Problems, decisions, and how you handled those decisions.
- What you have learned from your choices.
- Accomplishments.
- Strengths as you see them.
- Weaknesses as you see them.

It would be difficult to create an effective resumé and cover letter or conduct a winning interview if you haven't taken the time to organize essential information for your resumé and job application. Having information in one place will save you hours as you fill out applications and complete a resumé. You can update this data throughout your career.

Identification

Last name   First   Middle   Social security no.

Date/Place of birth

Present address

City   State   Zip

Phone (home)   Business phone
(   )   (   )

Previous or permanent address

In case of emergency, notify:
Name   Relationship

Address

Phone   Business Phone
(   )   (   )

Education

Primary—Name/Location

Years attended

High school—Name/Location

Years attended   Date graduated

College/Technical

Years attended   Date graduated

Other

Major

Subjects of special study

Business machines/equipment you can operate

Specific training, seminars

School Subjects and Activities

What subjects did you like best and why?

What extracurricular activities were you most involved in and which did you most enjoy and excel in?

Did you form good working relationships with teachers, administrators, and students? Explain.

Work Experience

List your complete employment record.

Employer—Name/Address
_____

Job title
_____

Duties
_____

Name of supervisor
_____

Dates
_____

Reason for leaving
_____

Internships
_____

Duties
_____

Name of supervisor
_____

Dates
_____

Volunteer work
_____

Duties
_____

Dates
_____

Workstudy/Part-time jobs
_____

Duties
_____

Supervisor
_____

Dates
_____

Military Experience

Dates
_____

Rank
_____

Duties
_____

Education or training
_____

References

Name
_____

Address
_____

Phone
_____

Years known
_____

What strengths do you bring to your job search? What are weaknesses that you need to face and overcome?

Examples of strengths	Examples of weaknesses
Self-starter	Little work experience
Positive attitude	Weak presentation skills
Good communication skills	Unemployed
Willing to learn	Frequent job changer
Solid education	Little training

Strengths	Weaknesses
_____	_____
_____	_____
_____	_____
_____	_____

Discover Your Strengths, Weaknesses, and Skills

Another goal of self-assessment is to discover your strengths, weaknesses, and skills in an effort to see what jobs you might be best suited for and in what areas you might want to improve. Review your autobiography, your list of accomplishments, and your database. What strengths and abilities have helped you through your life so far? What qualities or personal strengths helped you achieve your accomplishments? Win awards? Succeed in school or in other jobs? When did you make unsound decisions that you later regretted? What did you learn from them? Were there times in your life when you ignored problems or chose the quick solution? Look at these experiences honestly and determine what the real problem was, the weaknesses you observed, and the lessons you learned.

You can also discover your strengths by examining the skills you've acquired throughout your life.

Skills can be divided into two broad categories: job skills and transferable skills. Job skills are specialized and generally learned through study, on-the-job training, or job experience. They involve specific knowledge and enable you to perform a specific type of job, such as fixing a car or cooking a meal. Transferable skills are general skills that can be used and transferred to many jobs. Employers look for candidates who have *both* specific job skills and transferable skills.

Examples of Job Skills

Working with computers

Typing

Gardening

Overhauling an engine

Painting a house

Wallpapering

Bookkeeping

Cooking

Plumbing

Repairing equipment

Examples of Transferable Skills

Communicating

Problem solving

Critical thinking

Creativity

Interpreting

Organizing

Persuading

Managing

Negotiating

Analyzing

Using numbers

Connecting Skills with Interests

Generally, your skills match your interests. There are exceptions, however. You may be very good at computer skills, but sitting at a computer for eight hours leaves you cold. For most people, skills and interests fall into five areas. Knowing your skill area is helpful in narrowing down your choice of career areas. Few people fit into just one area. In fact, you may find you have interests in all five. Which of the following job skills and transferable skills do you have the most interest in?

People skills: You like to work with people to help, train, cure, develop, inform, and interact. You are a team player and are sensitive to the feelings of others. Examples: counselor or teacher.

Information or data skills: You like to work with data, details, and clerical information. Examples: computer programmer or secretary.

Mechanical skills: You prefer to work with machines, tools, plants, animals, and objects or to work outdoors. Examples: forester or veterinarian.

Creative skills: You have artistic, creative, or intuitive skills and like unstructured, imaginative, innovative situations. You are a creative problem solver. Examples: artist or writer.

Motivational skills: You like to work with people, motivating, persuading, influencing, or leading them for organization or economic gain. You like to solve problems and make decisions in a logical and systematic way. Examples: public speaker or administrator.

Look at your autobiography and database and notice the skills you have demonstrated. List them:

Strengths	Weaknesses	Skills	Interests
_____	_____	_____	_____
_____	_____	_____	_____
_____	_____	_____	_____
_____	_____	_____	_____
_____	_____	_____	_____

What's Your Style?

You will accomplish more at school and at work when you understand your natural learning and working style. Each side, or hemisphere, of the brain specializes in certain functions.   The left side is the center of language, logic, structure, organization, rational and linear thinking, analysis, sequencing of information, seriousness, and knowledge. The right side of the brain is the center of imagination, creativity, color, rhythm and music, daydreaming, spontaneity, intuition, and the arts. If you are stimulated by games and activities, like to take risks, and enjoy socializing, you are a right-brain dominant person. If you like solitude and quiet, are organized, like to work on tasks step-by-step, and feel more comfortable in familiar surroundings, you are a left-brain dominant person. Understanding which side of the brain you favor makes it easier to understand your working style.

Left-Brain Work Style

Have neat, organized work area

Have daily schedules

Work on one project at a time

Work alone

Work consistently

Like to plan work

Right-Brain Work Style

Have cluttered desk

Have flexible work times

Jump from project to project

Work with others

Work in bursts of energy

Procrastinate

In Chapter 8 we'll see how you can integrate both sides of the brain to increase your effectiveness. Your personality and team style is also connected to your brain dominance.

The following exercise will give you a sense of your dominant and preferred personality and team style. Understanding more about your style and how you relate to others can help you decide which career is best suited for you. This exercise is not meant to put you in a rigid category, but to indicate a general preference.

Many of these words could apply to you in certain situations. However, check the *one* word in each pair of words that best describes you. Then place a check mark on the corresponding line to the right. For example, check either Persuasive (under D) or Analytical (under T).

		D Director	R Relator	T Thinker	C Creator
1.	Persuasive	_____			
	Analytical			_____	
2.	Harmonious		_____		
	Logical			_____	
3.	Outgoing				_____
	Decisive	_____			
4.	Creative				_____
	Approachable		_____		
5.	Careful			_____	
	Independent	_____			
6.	Confident	_____			
	Idealistic				_____
7.	Receptive		_____		
	Enthusiastic				_____
8.	Action-oriented	_____			
	Thoughtful		_____		
9.	Loyal			_____	
	Flexible				_____
10.	Steady			_____	
	Informal		_____		
11.	Open		_____		
	Self-starter	_____			
12.	Personable				_____
	Factual			_____	
13.	Tactful		_____		
	Imaginative				_____
14.	Dedicated			_____	
	Energetic				_____
15.	Sensitive		_____		
	Imaginative				_____
16.	Competitive	_____			
	Cautious			_____	
17.	Innovative				_____
	Disciplined			_____	

(continued)

	D Director	R Relator	T Thinker	C Creator
18. Dynamic Detail-oriented	_____		_____	
19. Service-oriented Recognition		_____		_____
20. Hasty Thorough	_____		_____	
21. Spontaneous Planned			_____	_____
22. Objective Sympathetic	_____	_____		
23. Risk taking Supportive	_____	_____		
24. Popular Leader	_____	_____		
Totals	_____	_____	_____	_____

    To determine your style, add up the number of words checked in each category. For example, if you checked the most words in the D category, you have a dominant director style; if you checked the most words in the R list, you have a dominant relator style; if you checked the most words in the T list, you have a dominant thinker style; and if you checked the most words in the C list, you have a dominant creator style. The form styles, (D, R, T and C) are explained on page 18.

Director Style

A person with a dominant director's style tends to be confident, self-directed, energetic, dynamic, decisive, a risk taker, and results oriented. The director senses information immediately and makes quick decisions. A person with this style is a natural leader and likes to delegate responsibilities, organize and control situations, initiate action, and set and meet deadlines. Directors are task oriented, can motivate others, and like to be in charge.

Possible careers: Salesperson, motivational speaker, business owner, supervisor, manager, political campaigner, realtor, sports promoter, television producer, and lawyer. Directors like action.

Relator Style

A person with a dominant relator style tends to be sensitive, open, sympathetic, tactful, harmonious, approachable, caring, and a team player. This type of person operates through feelings and emotions and values helping others. The relator is a good listener, likes to encourage others, and has excellent people skills. The relator gains insight mainly through the right brain. The relator likes people.

Possible careers: Speech therapist, marriage and family counselor, psychologist, social worker, nurse, medical assistant, elderly patient care, community leader, teacher, and playground director. Relators like harmony.

Thinker Style

A person with a dominant thinker style tends to be exact, steady, careful, factual, organized, cautious, and loyal and likes rules, order, and established ways of doing things. The thinker gains insight through the left brain and likes accuracy.

Possible careers: Bookkeeper, accountant, computer operator, researcher, computer programmer, financial analyst, traffic controller, researcher, electrician, scientist, laboratory worker, meteorologist, engineer, and tax expert. Some thinkers are more rugged, outdoor types and prefer to work in agriculture, skilled trades, construction work, mechanics, forestry, or wildlife management. Thinkers are quiet, independent, and like to work with their hands.

Creator Style

A person with a dominant creator style tends to be creative, enthusiastic, spontaneous, innovative, flexible, original, and imaginative. The creator is intuitive, expressive, and gains insight through the right brain.

Possible careers: Artist, cartoonist, composer, singer, dramatic coach, salesperson, interior designer, travel guide, and writer. Creators who are more extroverted may go into sales, public relations, reporting, or public speaking. Creators like original ideas.

Uncover Your Values

Self-assessment also helps you define your values. Values are the emotional reasons for which we commit our time and energy. Values are the "why's" of life and are what make a job fulfilling, satisfying, and inherently valuable to you. Values need to be given high priority in deciding on a career or a job. Some people value freedom, time off, or status more than a high salary. No one can give you the "right" values. Only you can determine what is right for you. Do you prefer jobs that let you

- Help others?
- Make lots of money?
- Have freedom?
- Live where you want to?
- Have flexible work hours?
- Be creative?
- Supervise others?
- Work alone?
- Work with details?
- See the big picture?

- Take risks?
- Work outdoors?
- Achieve fulfillment and potential?
- Use power and authority?
- Gain recognition?
- Solve problems?
- Learn new skills?
- Be a recognized expert?
- Spend a lot of time with your family?

To clarify your values, take a moment to review the key points in your life that you wrote about earlier. Look at your autobiography and study the situations in which you achieved recognition or pushed yourself to achieve a goal. When you have reviewed your life for patterns, consider these questions:

- What experiences brought me the most joy and satisfaction?
- What values are most important in my job?
- Is it important to make a contribution to the world or to help society in my job?
- Do I want to help people by working in small groups or directly on a one-to-one basis?
- Is it important for me to make decisions or influence people?
- Is interesting, creative work essential to my happiness, or can I find my creative expression outside my job?
- Do I need security, independence, variety, prestige, excitement, artistic involvement?
- Do I want job security or am I a risk taker?

Next, jot down your thoughts:
The top three values that are most important in a job are

_____

_____

_____

The rewards that are most important to me are

_____

_____

_____

Exploring Careers and Making a Match

Now that you have assessed your interests, skills, strengths, and values, it is time to explore careers. Since you will be spending much of your time at work, it is important that you choose a career that you'll love and that you can succeed in. In Chapter 2, researching and networking will be covered. Both can help you explore what careers are growing and what skills and qualities are necessary to succeed in certain jobs. Do your interests and skills fit into any of these fastest-growing careers?

Fastest Growing Jobs
1992–2005

Fastest Growing Occupations Requiring a Bachelor's Degree:
Percent employment growth of occupations requiring a college degree, projected 1992–2005

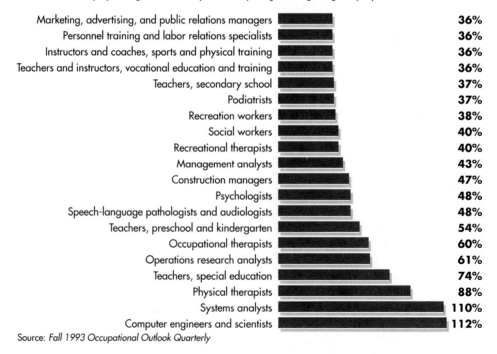

Marketing, advertising, and public relations managers	36%
Personnel training and labor relations specialists	36%
Instructors and coaches, sports and physical training	36%
Teachers and instructors, vocational education and training	36%
Teachers, secondary school	37%
Podiatrists	37%
Recreation workers	38%
Social workers	40%
Recreational therapists	40%
Management analysts	43%
Construction managers	47%
Psychologists	48%
Speech-language pathologists and audiologists	48%
Teachers, preschool and kindergarten	54%
Occupational therapists	60%
Operations research analysts	61%
Teachers, special education	74%
Physical therapists	88%
Systems analysts	110%
Computer engineers and scientists	112%

Source: *Fall 1993 Occupational Outlook Quarterly*

THE FASTEST GROWING JOBS

1. Information Technology The entire field of information technology will offer the fastest-growing occupations. Computer engineers and scientists will grow by 112 percent by the year 2000. There will also be a growing number of opportunities in network services or systems. For example, one hot job will be an on-line multimedia content developer. This is a professional who will infuse products with textual, visual, and audio life.

By the year 2000, software programming jobs will have grown by more than 30 percent to more than 700,000. Programmers are needed in almost all industries to program a variety of systems. As CD-ROMs continue to be the fastest-growing segment of the $20 billion-a-year software industry, multimedia training will be highly prized.

A systems analyst is a programmer who specializes in corporate databases to project needs, solve problems, and reach goals. By 2000, the number of systems analysts will increase by over 100 percent.

2. Electronic Communications Professionals, such as on-line services marketers, will work in the field to train users with the software and to monitor customer relations. This will be a growing field as electronic communications continues to grow. Related careers include customer support jobs and sales.

3. Health Care Professionals Health care is projected to grow by 47 percent by the year 2000 and will move out of hospitals and into community- and home-based settings. Physical therapists, geriatric care managers, and nurse practitioners (registered nurses with advanced training) will be growing specialties. The field of physical therapy will increase by 88 percent by the year 2000. Related careers include athletic and physical trainers and exercise physiologists. There will also be a growing need for speech-language pathologists and audiologists, and occupational therapists. The need for health assistance for an aging population will also increase. Geriatric care managers are social workers or nurses who work for families to provide care for the elderly. By 2000, almost 36 million people will be 65 or older.

4. Human Services The helping professions will increase by 70 percent by the year 2000. Corporate human service occupations include human resources managers; professionals; labor relations specialists; employee assistance program counselors; marketing, advertising, and planned giving officers. These professionals offer assessment skills and expertise in treatment, training, compensation, and diversity management. Other industry focus areas will include customer service, public relations, and fundraising.

5. Teachers Part of the growth in the area of the helping professions will be a growing need for teachers, both at the elementary and secondary level. Special-education teachers will be most in demand to work with developmentally disabled, physically impaired, or emotionally disturbed children. Other growing occupations in the helping professions field will include psychologists, counselors, occupational therapists, and social workers.

6. Financial Services The investment service area will see a growth in such occupations as portfolio managers, trust managers, bank financial-service marketers, and independent financial planners. Professional women are the fastest growing investors in the personal-finance industry.

7. Travel and Tourism The travel and tourism industry is expected to increase by 30 percent by the year 2000. There will be a growing need for hotel managers, leisure-time managers, destination marketers, tourism managers, tour guides and travel agents.

8. Environment Those in industry will continue to hire consultants and engineers to help them comply with environmental regulations. Such occupations are environmental engineers, managers specializing in environmental ethics, and geographic information systems practitioners. GIS practitioners combine computerized mapping with data analysis to determine environmental issues such as where to put a waste facility.

9. Law Growth occupations in law include paralegals, legal assistants, law-firm marketers, labor and employment lawyers, property lawyers, and environmental attorneys. More companies are hiring attorneys to help translate complex labor laws and comply with new rules and regulations.

10. Corrections Corrections and security professionals will increase to help prevent crime. These careers will include corrections officers, counselors, health care providers, computer-security specialists, high-tech security guards, and white-collar crime law-enforcement experts.

Develop Your Personal Qualities, Attitude, and Self-Esteem

People are hired for many reasons. Sometimes candidates demonstrate specific skills that the organization needs. In other cases, the employer wants a person who can solve problems; make sound decisions; is a team player; or has a motivated, enthusiastic attitude. One thing is clear: Personal qualities such as a positive attitude, initiative, honesty, willingness to work hard, loyalty, creativity, the ability to solve problems, and willingness to learn are often even more important than education or technical skills.

In Chapter 7 we'll look at how important personal qualities are for career success.

The Role of Self-Esteem

How you feel about yourself can affect you at every stage of the job-search process and can directly affect your success on the job. The attitude you bring to any task is reflected in everything you do. A person with high self-esteem is confident and self-reliant and has self-respect, skills, and a sense of basic worthiness. Having a positive self-image and feeling confident and competent can also increase your motivation. Self-respect leads to integrity and fosters the ability to communicate in a direct and aboveboard style. Therefore, developing high self-esteem can help you be more successful in your career.

Characteristics of people with high self-esteem include

- A willingness to learn new skills.
- Self-trust.
- The ability to be self-directed.
- A sense of competency.
- A resistance to dependencies and addictions.
- The ability to cope with stress, adversity, and problems.
- A basic sense of well-being and happiness.

Characteristics of people with low self-esteem include

- A basic feeling of unworthiness and lack of self-respect.
- The inability to form solid, healthy relationships.
- Vulnerability to peer pressure and lack of inner trust.
- The tendency to abuse drugs or alcohol or to have eating disorders.
- Lack of confidence in ability to perform in school or at work.
- A basic feeling of hopelessness and unhappiness.

Knowing yourself through self-assessment will help you set goals and work out a plan for learning new skills and overcoming weaknesses. It will also prepare you for the task of writing your resumé and shining during the interview and will help you organize and give structure to your job-search process. You will be in a good position to creatively explore options and begin using critical thinking to help make solid choices about your career.

Creating a Positive Attitude

Do you see the job-search process as a boring, frustrating, and discouraging process that you will drop as soon as you get the first job that comes along? Or do you approach the job search with a sense of adventure and see it as an ongoing process that involves exploring, investigating, and discovering more about yourself and your career? If your attitude is negative, it could sabotage your chances of job success. It will also decrease your energy, and you may become discouraged. If your attitude is positive, people will want to brainstorm job opportunities with you and will feel good about recommending you for jobs. You will also have the strength to handle setbacks.

A positive attitude is fundamental to job success. Whether or not you project confidence, enthusiasm, an upbeat approach, and have assertive communication skills will make an enormous difference in how others see you. These are the qualities that you have control over and that you can make work for you. They are also the very qualities that are so important in being successful on the job. Successful people are positive people. They know they are responsible for their attitudes and behaviors and know they have the power to change them at any time. Negative people feel they are victims of circumstances and blame others for their unmotivated state of mind. It is important to be able to overcome the frustrations and discouragement that are part of the job-search process and of life itself. Two strategies that can make a big difference in your attitude and self-esteem are self-talk and imagery.

POSITIVE

NEGATIVE

Self-Talk, Self-Image, and Imagery

What you say to yourself all day and the mental images that you create have a powerful effect on your attitude. The messages you tell yourself can program you to be more energetic, enthusiastic, and goal directed. Positive self-talk and images can improve your attitude and self-image and can empower you. Negative self-talk can send you into a self-sabotaging downward spiral.

For example, you may wake up one morning and say, I don't want to prepare for this job interview. I am very shy and uncomfortable in interviews. I know I'll blow it. It's no use anyway. There are no good jobs out there. I might as well go back to sleep.

Self-talk is usually accompanied by images. In the above example, you may see yourself failing in a job interview and may actually get butterflies just thinking about talking with employers. Imagery is just that—imagining yourself in certain situations, talking and behaving in either a positive or negative way. These images can produce confidence, enthusiasm, and success, or they can focus on fear, worry, and failure. As with self-talk, your mental images can go unnoticed unless you consciously stop and assess them.

You can learn to choose positive thoughts, self-talk, and imagery and improve your attitude. By changing your behavior, you can take charge of your career. Positive self-talk and images can help you overcome doubt, increase your confidence and self-esteem, and help you focus on completion and success.

EXERCISE 1.5 Improve Your Self-Talk, Self-Image, and Imagery

Most people are unaware of the steady stream of negative thoughts, self-talk, and images that go through their minds every day. For now, don't try to change your thoughts; just observe and record them in a detached manner.

1. Assess your self-talk and imagery for a few hours. Write down all your negative and positive self-talk and imagery.

Positive self-talk   Negative self-talk

Positive imagery   Negative imagery

2. Translate your self-talk and imagery from negative to positive.

For example:

Negative: *I will never get a job. The economy is bad, and there are too many people to compete with. I am afraid of rejection.*

Positive: *I am confident and self-assured. I am putting in time every day to assess my values, abilities, skills, and likes and to explore careers.*

(continued)

3. What attitudes or personality traits would you consider important for success in a job? By changing your attitude, you can produce the results you want in all areas of your life. Here are a few qualities that many employers say are important.

- Imagination.
- Creativity.
- Ingenuity.
- Critical thinking skills.
- Intelligence without a "know-it-all" attitude.
- Persuasiveness.
- Ability to relate to difficult people.
- Ability to be calm and cool-headed in crisis.
- Good communication skills.
- Ability to adapt to change.
- Willingness to learn.
- Disciplined work habits.
- Ability to follow through.
- Ability to bounce back when down.
- Ability to focus on correcting rather than blaming.
- Positive attitude.
- Enthusiasm and energy.
- Ability to be a self-starter.
- Problem-solving abilities.
- Other_____

4. Review your autobiography for times in your life when you were positive, enthusiastic, and motivated. When did you push yourself to achieve a goal? Perhaps it was achieving an award in speech, debate or drama club; running for school office; Girl or Boy Scouts; or excelling in a sporting event.

a. Describe how you felt, your body language, self-talk, and so on.

b. What do you consider your most valuable attitudes and personal qualities?

c. List times in your life when you've demonstrated a few of the above personal qualities. Which of these attitudes and personal qualities would you use in your ideal job?

d. What is your attitude toward work? What do you like and dislike about work? Once you start exploring the good things about having a job, you can become clear on why you want a job.

Like   Dislike

Image Counts

It only takes a few minutes for others to form either a positive or negative first impression of you. As the old saying goes, "You never get a second chance to create a good first impression." Careers are made and lost based on first impressions. Therefore, throughout the job search process, you will want to create a first impression that reveals a confident, neat, well-groomed, friendly, and professional image. Your appearance, dress, body language, tone of voice, and eye contact all combine to create an image that communicates your style. Never underestimate the power of image.

Take the time to honestly assess your image and appearance and set goals that will help you put it all together in a winning way. Appearance refers to the the total visual impression you make and takes into account clothing, shoes, hair, accessories, nails, makeup, eye contact, body type, posture, body language, smells, and color. If you are going to school, you may not see the need to start thinking about image. No one expects you to dress as if you were a top executive. However, you can dress for school and still begin to build a professional wardrobe. If you are working part-time, have an internship, are in a co-op program, or even doing volunteer work, you should dress in a professional and appropriate style. By assessing your image, you can be more aware of what image you are projecting now and how you want to look as a career professional. Ask yourself these questions:

- Is my clothing professional and appropriate for the job? Do I have one basic, suit or suitable outfit for interviews?
- Are my clothing and shoes neat, clean, stylish, and of good quality?
- Are my nails, hairstyle, makeup, perfume/cologne, and color scheme, flattering, neat, professional looking, and in good taste?
- Are accessories, such as jewelry, ties/scarfs, briefcase, and pen, professionallooking?

We will talk more about the importance of first impressions in Chapter 5.

THE BENEFIT FACTOR

The Benefit Factor

Most people focus on what they want rather than focusing on what an employer wants. Throughout this book, you will be asked how you can benefit the employer. Successfully communicating what you have to offer is what really gets you the job. Self-assessment is not just a soul-searching activity, but the foundation for your job search and success in your career. It can help you organize your questions, match your skills with the company's needs, and structure your job-search process in a systematic and businesslike manner. You need to know enough about yourself to be honest about your skills, knowledge, experience, interests, and aptitude. *Then* you need to determine how best to market yourself to get and keep an interesting job where you can contribute your talents. Ask yourself these questions:

- What do I have to offer an employer?
- What could I do to benefit a company?
- What do I have that would satisfy a need for a company?

- How can I demonstrate that I have problem-solving skills, can make sound decisions, and can work well as a team member?
- What have I achieved, and how is this demonstrated?

As you will see, an employee who has a good sense of strengths, weaknesses, and skills, who is flexible, and who can adjust to change is a benefit to the company.

THE REVOLUTIONARY WORKPLACE

Workplace Trends

Key: Change

In the last decade, the American workplace has undergone a revolution. Not since the beginning of mass production has there been such a radical redefinition of workplace norms. These changes will affect how people see their jobs and how they define work.

A global economy, rapidly evolving technology, and higher costs are creating a massive paradigm shift.

Intense global competition requires greater efficiency and more productivity in American businesses. Downsizing, restructuring, and reengineering are just a few of the measures that have resulted in fewer jobs. Layers of hierarchical business structure have been cut; there is a widening gulf between the haves and have-nots; employees are working harder for less money and fewer benefits; management must tackle social and health problems associated with drugs, alcohol, and AIDS; and the white male culture is slowly becoming multicultural.

The worker of today must be willing to adapt to change and successfully navigate in this shaky corporate terrain. How employees react to these changes will determine, to a degree, their level of job satisfaction.

Career Strategies: Learn flexibility and sensitivity; develop an optimistic attitude and the ability to embrace change. The global economy has emerged as many nations and cultures become increasingly interdependent.

HITTING THE WALL

Scaling the Wall

Few job hunters are prepared for the amount of work and time required for a successful job search. Even after being told that looking for a job is a full-time job, many think they will be the exception to the rule. Be prepared to make a total commitment. The job-hunting process can be a lengthy and difficult task and needs to be taken seriously. Job hunting, like life, is not fair. You may know of someone who was hired even though he or she was less qualified than other applicants. You may not have been hired for a job even though you were very well qualified. You may have also noticed that people are sometimes promoted or not promoted based on reasons other than ability or competence. Some people seem to have a knack for creating really good resumés and can create a spark during the interview process even though they may be weak on experience. Some people keep a job for years, until they decide to leave, while others are forced into the job-hunting process overnight through no fault of their own.

Be prepared for moments of self-doubt and discouragement—just learn how to overcome these feelings.

Hurdling the Barriers

The major difference between a successful job hunter and a person who doesn't get hired is that the successful person invests time and thought in planning the search. Here is a strategy to apply when your energy dips:

Start the Day Off Right

Set the alarm a few minutes early to allow yourself to slowly wake up. While you are still in this relaxed state, review your priorities for the day and see yourself achieving them. One of the most effective times to use imaging and positive self-talk (affirmation) is when you first awaken and the mind is very relaxed and open to reprogramming. An affirmation is a positive statement that helps reprogram the mind to produce positive results.

See yourself efficiently accomplishing your day's main goals. See yourself with a high level of confidence and a center of calm. You are quietly going through your day, completing each priority. After a hot shower and a few minutes of yoga, stretching exercises, or aerobics, review your affirmations while you're getting dressed. Here are a few affirmations. Write several of your own.

- I can see the importance of each step in the job-search process.
- When I am involved in a tasks, I am fully absorbed.
- I wake up each day with a sense of anticipation and purpose.

The Knockout Factor

- Not taking time for self-reflection and assessment.
- Being negative and discouraged.
- Being inactive.
- Not planning.
- Not relating skills to your accomplishments.

The Success Factor

- Taking time for assessment, goal setting, and dreaming.
- Creating and maintaining a positive and motivating attitude.
- Taking control of the job-search process by being action-oriented.
- Preparing and planning.
- Relating skills to your accomplishments.

PROBLEM SOLVING AT WORK

Problem Solving

Tom has always loved working with people. He is an extroverted, action-oriented type and enjoys being the center of attention. He is also a good organizer. Tom likes to motivate others and manage events and activities. He is a natural leader. He coordinated an outstanding campaign in high school that resulted in his being elected president of his senior class. He also loves the outdoors and is an avid camper and hiker.

Tom entered a small private college with a major in business. His family operates an accounting business in a large city, and he will have a job waiting for him when he finishes college. Tom's father is an accountant, and it has always been assumed that Tom would become a CPA and take over the company when his father retired. However, after taking several general education courses and reflecting on his interests, goals, and values, Tom has decided that he does not want to sit behind a desk every day. Nor does he want to put in the required long hours at tax time. Tom is considering a career in forestry so he can enjoy the outdoors and go on camping trips. However, he also wants to make a good living and have a secure job, and he likes the challenge of the business world. He would like to own his own business.

You can see Tom's problem. Should he get an accounting degree that would ensure him a good job and please his parents, or should he explore a job in forestry? Here is how Tom used creative problem solving to explore solutions and critical thinking to make a sound decision.

1. Have I clearly stated the problems? Should I major in accounting or forestry?

2. Do I have enough information? Should I research the forestry field and talk with forestry professionals? Do I know the job forecast, average salaries, and what foresters really do?

3. Can I make the decision by myself? What resources are available to help me make a better decision? Have I talked with a career counselor, my advisor, my parents?

4. Have I brainstormed alternatives? What other jobs are available in the business field? Would a career in sales or public relations combine my skills with my interests? What other jobs might I want to explore?

5. Have I looked at likely consequences? If I change majors, will I have to go to school longer? If I go into forestry, will there be fewer job opportunities, as well as less advancement or pay? Would I miss the opportunities and advantages that a big city offers? Would I be resentful if I became an accountant?

6. Have I identified all the resources and tools needed? Have I researched the requirements of a forestry major. Do I have the necessary math skills? Am I willing to acquire the additional skills and tools to be successful?

7. Have I developed and implemented an action plan? Have I designed a plan that will help me make a sound decision? Have I assessed my interests, skills, values, and goals?

8. Have I identified the best solution and done everything possible to ensure success? Have I made a decision using critical thinking and creativity? Am I committed to making the decision a success?

9. Have I assessed the results? Have I evaluated my decision to see if it is working? Have I assessed my grades, work satisfaction, and goals?

10. Have I modified the plan, if necessary? What adjustments could I make that would make my decision more successful?

Self-Assessment Strategies

- Take time to plan, reflect, and get organized.
- Be flexible, persistent, and creative.
- Communicate your goals, abilities, and skills.
- Be confident and positive.
- Create a sense of high self-esteem.
- Assess your values and life's purpose.
- Assess your skills, abilities, and personal qualities.
- Become a creative problem solver.
- Remember: A job search is a full-time job.
- Use critical thinking to make sound decisions.

Chapter Checklist   Yes   No

1. Have you reflected and thought about the kind of job you want?

2. Have you assessed the skills you have?

3. Have you assessed your personal qualities?

4. Have you assessed your values and what is most important to you in life?

5. Have you taken time to dream about the job you would really like?

6. Have you assessed your interests?

7. Have you assessed your problem-solving abilities?

8. Have you assessed examples of using critical thinking to make sound decisions?

9. Have you assessed your education and training and what areas you excel in?

10. Have you assessed your work experience and the jobs you have enjoyed most?

11. Have you assessed the areas in which you need to improve and learn new skills?

12. Have you assessed your sense of self-worth?

13. Have you adopted ways to increase your self-esteem?

14. Have you assessed your attitude?

CHAPTER 2

Exploring Job Options and Networking

If you have built castles in the air, your work need not be lost; that is where they should be. Now put foundations under them.

Henry David Thoreau

Participation in a professional network is a valuable activity that will help you, not only in your search for your first position, but throughout your career as well.

Mary M. Heiberger and
Julia M. Vick
The Academic Job Search Handbook

Introduction

Just as you learned the value of reflection in Chapter 1, you will now learn the importance of action. We will look at specific strategies for setting goals, researching jobs, and exploring creative ways to find jobs, and at the importance of networking and internships. You'll see that networking is not only a part of job research, but also an ongoing career skill.

—

Learning Objectives

In Chapter 2, you will learn

* The importance of setting goals.

* How to set goals.

* How to research jobs in a traditional way.

* How to research jobs in a nontraditional way.

* How to network.

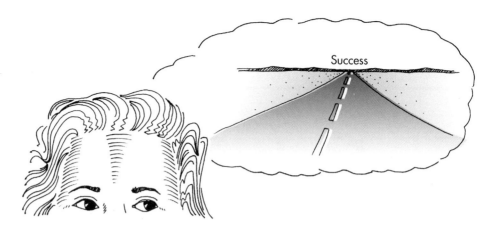

Focus Your Job Search: Set Goals

Now that you have assessed your strengths, weaknesses, attitudes, needs, values, and interests; learned strategies for creatively solving problems; and understand the importance of critical thinking in decision making, you are ready to focus your job search and to set goals. A major reason that some job searchers become sidetracked and discouraged is that they lack goals. They may not have devoted much time to thinking about what they would really like to do. They may have drifted into a major or career as a result of a part-time job; joined the family business; or gotten into a certain career because of the opportunities, money, or status. Other people may resist setting goals because they think goals will lock them into certain decisions. It is important to remember that a goal is simply a guide. A goal is like a road map: It gives you a sense of direction. You can change your direction and destination at any time.

You will find it easier to keep a positive attitude and maintain high energy if you have a focus for your job search. Some job searchers feel discouraged even though they have been working hard and involved with lots of activity, because their efforts have been scattered and disorganized, producing few results.

Goals help you

1. Clarify what you want and determine specific results.
2. Gain a sense of direction, energy, and focus.
3. Gain a feeling of accomplishment and competency.
4. Produce results by doing first things first.
5. Have a more positive attitude and increased self-esteem.

Goal-Setting Steps

1. Determine what you want to accomplish. The first step is to determine what you want to accomplish. Goals should be put in writing, prioritized, and reviewed often. A goal that is not written is just a wish or dream. Write a specific job objective that you want to achieve now. Then expand your thinking and set long-term goals. Start with 1-year, 5-year, and 10-year goals. Then write down your lifetime goals. Remember, these can be revised and changed as your circumstances, experience, and opportunities change.

2. Establish a time line. Next, allocate a certain amount of time for both your long- and short-term goals. Set a year-long time line and monthly and weekly target dates. Creating a time line for accomplishing your goals helps align everyday actions with your long-term goals and your life's purpose. It also helps you visualize what needs to be done and when it should be accomplished.

3. Set Priorities. To be a successful job searcher, you need to learn to do first things first. Setting daily priorities by using a "to-do list" will help you put abstract goals into immediate action. Each day, begin with a list of tasks to be achieved. Review your list to make certain the tasks are related to your goals and are not just frantic activity. You need to allocate enough time to ensure that you are doing important things, things that lead to accomplishing your goals. Prioritize each task by assigning it an A for most important, B for next important, and so on. Make it a daily habit to start with first things first and work through your list.

	Job Search To-Do List		
Goals	Priorities	To See or Call	
		Awaiting Developments	
		What	Who	When
Continuing Attention Items			

4. Assess results. Periodically evaluate your progress. Assess the results of your activity and determine what factors are contributing to your success and what factors are wasting time. Are you spending your high-energy time on your most important goals? Or are you doing the easiest tasks first and spending leftover time on high-priority tasks? You may need to assess your day and adopt new, positive habits that will help you to overcome procrastination and achieve the results you want.

Goal-Setting Tips:

- Take time to plan and reflect.
- Put your goals in writing.
- Write specific goals.
- Write both short- and long-term goals.
- Assess the benefits of reaching your goals.
- Determine which goals overlap.
- Determine which goals are incompatible.
- Establish a schedule and time line.
- Set specific deadlines for accomplishing your goals.
- Establish daily priorities and tasks, and break large goals into small tasks.
- Do first things first.
- Consolidate similar tasks.
- Use idle time to accomplish tasks.
- Learn to say no to distractions and to stay on target.
- Overcome procrastination: Just get started.
- Review goals and progress often.
- Reward yourself for accomplishing your goals.

Haven't a Clue?

If you still don't know what you want to do, skip Exercise 2.1, explore the careers section in this chapter (Researching Jobs and Informational Interviews), and then come back to the exercise. Don't worry if you have trouble writing a clear and specific goal. It is not an easy task. Many people find they need previous job experience to give them direction and help them sort through all the job possibilities. Getting started is the biggest step. You'll find that you can fine-tune your goal statement as you go through your job search. The more practice you have in writing goals, the easier it gets.

My immediate job objective is

_____

My major goal this year is

_____

My major goal in 5 years is

_____

My major goal in 10 years is

_____

Other life goals are

_____

The most important goal in my life, or my life's purpose, is

_____

Goal Assessment

After you have thought about your goals, answer these questions:

How important is your major goal?

Is your major goal in conflict with your other goals?

Which goals are top priorities?

How do you feel about achieving your major goal?

What are the benefits to achieving your major goal?

What alternatives are available if you don't achieve your major goal?

How do your goals relate to your life's purpose and your values?

Are your goals realistic?

What barriers might you have to overcome to achieve your goals?

What resources are available to help you achieve your goals?

Action Plan

What smaller steps are necessary to reach your major goal and objective?
For example: **Major goal:** To graduate from college. **Action plan:** (1) Pick up
college schedule; (2) Talk with an advisor; (3) Enroll in a class.

1.

2.

3.

4. etc.

Keep an action form, like the one on page 38, to monitor your progress.

Barriers

What barriers could prevent you from reaching your goal? Can you plan to overcome these barriers? For example: **Barrier to Overcome:** Lack of follow-through. **Solution:** I will keep a detailed checklist of each step necessary and review it every day to ensure that I follow through on each step.

    1.

    2.

    3. etc.

Here is a sample time line to help you plan your year. Modify it to fit your needs:

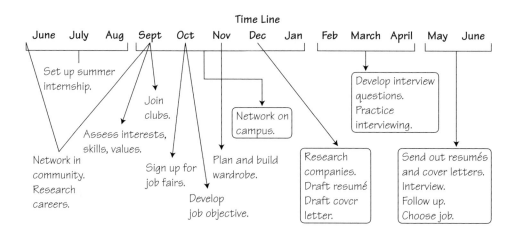

Time Line

| June | July | Aug | Sept | Oct | Nov | Dec | Jan | Feb | March | April | May | June |

Set up summer internship.

Join clubs.

Assess interests, skills, values.

Network in community. Research careers.

Sign up for job fairs.

Develop job objective.

Plan and build wardrobe.

Network on campus.

Research companies. Draft resumé Draft cover letter.

Develop interview questions. Practice interviewing.

Send out resumés and cover letters. Interview. Follow up. Choose job.

Date:	Weekly Job-Search Action Form		
Goal	Deadline	Completed	Notes
Complete resumé	October 23	October 21	Prepare list to send

    Once you've set goals and thought about what kind of job you'd like at this time in your life, the next step is to research where you can find this job.

Researching Jobs

Crucial to a successful job search is knowing how to research jobs and companies. There are two main paths for discovering what jobs are available. One is the traditional path of newspaper ads, advertisements, and employment agencies. But there are literally thousands of jobs in a variety of fields that take some creative exploring to uncover. Most are not listed in the classifieds, many are not advertised, and some may not have specific titles. In fact, it has been estimated that between 70 and 90 percent of the available jobs can be found in the hidden job market. The nontraditional path for exploring the job market includes networking through both professional and trade organizations and researching jobs through various publications. It is important to explore and research both the traditional and the nontraditional paths to ensure a successful job search.

Students who participate in professional and trade organizations will have a head start on building contacts and relationships. There is no substitute for the grapevine. You can find out which companies are growing, which have new products, and how frequently they hire or lay off employees.

Researching jobs through various publications is also important to do before you graduate. Articles can indicate which careers are growing. You can learn more about the market, key players, and new trends in particular fields. In addition, companies often list job announcements in trade journals. You can determine the employer's preference by noting style, key words, and expectations through job announcements. This information can help you put together a targeted resumé and cover letter and help you prepare for the interview.

Traditional Sources for the Job Search

Source #1: The Media

Newspapers

Few people get jobs by answering newspaper ads. However, you should still explore this source because it will give you information about companies,—who is hiring and what kinds of jobs are available,—and you may find jobs that you want to pursue. Don't just read a few local papers. Look at *The Wall Street Journal*, the *New York Times, National Employment Weekly,* and large newspapers in your area. Sunday papers are especially helpful.

In addition, read the business section for opportunity leads. Investigate companies that have hit new sales records, are developing new products, are expanding into new territory, or have merged with other companies. Look for articles about managers being promoted or employees who are leaving to take other jobs. This means the company will be going through some changes. These articles are, for your purposes, job ads and are worth following up with a cover letter and resumé or phone call.

You also may find a company that really appeals to you. Even if they say they are not hiring, it's worth a visit. Or you can send a cover letter and resumé to the head of the department in which you are interested. Don't worry if the ad is six months old. Most companies move very slowly with hiring, and most will consider an applicant even after the closing date has passed. All companies experience unplanned turnover, and if your letter or visit creates interest and demonstrates that you have done your homework, you may find yourself at the right spot at the right time.

TV and Radio

Listen to the news and you will find many stories about business successes, expansion, new productions, franchises, new growth in the community, and local job opportunities. There are also TV shows on job opportunities, such as specials on business trends and job forecasts.

Commercial spots on TV and radio will also give you a clue to which businesses are marketing their products and creating new products.

Source #2: Campus Recruiters

A school's recruitment program is not a major job source because only a few companies recruit on campus. However, you should explore this source to learn more about certain companies, to practice interviewing, and to explore various jobs within the company.

1. Start a file of job openings. Check out all campus and community job postings. The specific job may not appeal to you, but you may be interested in the company.

2. Talk to a company representative. This is a great way to learn more about the company. Get the name, title, and phone number of the company representative so you can follow up with more questions.

3. Keep a log of names. Ask for names and titles of the managers who head the departments in which you are most interested.

Source #3: Employment Agencies

Employment agencies can be effective in finding jobs. They can also help you with resumé writing and interviewing skills; help you assess your skills and interests; and help you match your skills and interests with available jobs. Employment agencies charge a fee, but it is often paid by the company that hires you. Look in the yellow pages for a list of employment agencies in your area.

Nontraditional Resources

Source #1: The library

The library is a treasure of information about available jobs, occupations, industries, and companies. Use the library as a traditional resource for looking through newspapers. Use it also as a nontraditional resource for research and for browsing through trade journals. Trade journals discuss new trends and also list professional organizations in related fields. Don't forget to investigate on-line resources as well as newspapers and magazines, which often highlight up-to-date job trends. Ask your librarian about accessing the Internet—a vast resource network with information about all types of industries, organizations, and job trends. Get to know your librarian, ask for specific trade journals, and check out the following:

The Dictionary of Occupational Titles
The Guide for Occupational Exploration
US Department of Labor Occupational Books
The Occupational Outlook Handbook
Almanac of American Employers
Business Periodical Index
Wall Street Journal Index
Dun & Bradstreet's Million Dollar Directory
Standard Industrial Classification
Career Placement Directory
College Placement Annual
Ulrich's International Periodical Directory
Gale Directory of Publications
Standard Periodical Directory
National Directory of Addresses and Telephone Numbers
Consultants and Consulting Organization Directory
Wall Street Journal
Washington Post
New York Times
Manufacturing directories
Trade journals and magazines

Phone Book

Most libraries have phone books from across the country. Look in the phone book both in the Yellow Pages under broad areas that interest you and in the business section. Make a list of the companies that you are most interested in and call them to request more information—annual reports, sales projections, brochures, growth projections, future plans, and so on.

Also use the phone book to look through the yellow pages for agencies that can help you research jobs. Here are a few resources that can help:

Career placement offices.

Civic clubs.

List of local businesses.

List of schools, colleges, and universities.

Employment agencies.

Employment security office (state or federal).

State job-service offices.

Source #2: The Community

Investigate the community. Find out who the mayor is and who local business leaders are, and look at the programs offered by the Rotary and Kiwanis Clubs. Keep a file marked "Community" and enclose information regarding company profiles and job opportunities from such community sources as:

Chamber of commerce directory.

Local directories of businesses.

Professional organizations.

Small Business Administration.

Rotaries.

Local college placement offices.

Source #3: Organizations

Investigate organizations. In the networking section of your job-search notebook, keep a file of clippings from newspapers and magazines and information you gather from organizations. Be sure to include annual reports, flyers, brochures, employee packages, applications, and telephone directories.

Source #4: Observation

Now that you have some leads, take your job search to the streets. Look for new businesses going up, new products being advertised, new buildings, or other signs of expansion. New products may indicate growth for a department, and the company may be hiring new employees. If you notice new branches of a business being built, write to the corporate headquarters or talk to the local manager. You will find new products on the shelf. By increasing your observation skills, you will find new products on the shelf and discover what businesses are growing.

Use the following guide to do the detective work necessary to find out what types of jobs are available.

A. Investigate the company. When you find a company that appeals to you, find out as much as you can about it. Request an annual report; find out about future plans and new products from the sales office. There may be great opportunities in new organizations or in small companies that are easy to overlook.

B. Ignore job specifications. A company may say they are looking for a candidate with a master's degree, a high grade-point average, a degree in a specific area, or a certain number of years of experience. Apply even if you don't meet all the stated requirements. If they are impressed with you, they may discuss other job opportunities.

C. Take action. Find out what jobs are open and to whom you would report. Call the department and tell the secretary you are going to be sending a letter (don't say resumé, or you may be directed to personnel) and that you want to check the spelling and title of the director of the office. Remember, you want to go directly to the person who has the authority to hire you.

D. Send a cover letter. Write a cover letter that describes your interest in the company, includes company information that indicates you have done extensive homework on them, and explains how you think you can benefit the company. Cover letters will be discussed in more detail in Chapter 4.

Source #5 Internships

Job experience is important to employers. Internships, cooperative education programs, and volunteering can give you experience, help you explore careers, and help you learn good job skills and habits. They are also wonderful ways to build contacts and get your foot in the door of a company. Internships are also a wonderful way to start networking while you are still in school.

Internships—paid or unpaid apprentice-type positions—are priceless. They are another way you can demonstrate that you can "hit the ground running." Students find internships valuable because they can link theory with real-world application. Many companies view internships as a recruiting tool. This experience gives employers the opportunity to actually try someone out, test his or her skills, and see if the person fits in. Especially in recession times or in tough competitive job markets, employers want graduates who have job experience. Not only do you gain valuable experience, you will be able to demonstrate to the employer that you took the initiative to research internships and learn more about the business world.

A successful internship can

- Place you in an entry-level job.
- Provide excellent firsthand experiences.
- Help you in career planning and decision making.
- Provide knowledge about the field and give you the opportunity to develop useful skills.
- Establish contacts with professional people.
- Provide an opportunity to gain greater responsibility.

The internship is, indeed, an important strategy for building a network, for career planning, and for getting a job. When you plan your internship, think about what you want to gain as well as what you can contribute. The following are questions to consider:

- What kind of work, responsibility, advancement, exposure, location, and possibility for job placement does it offer?
- Is it a paid internship? Does your school offer credit? Is there a grade-point requirement? Is it formally structured, or will you have some independence?
- Do you want to spend the summer in an internship, take a semester off school to intern full time, or intern part time?
- In what setting would you like to intern: urban area, rural area, resort, foreign country?

To find out what opportunities exist, talk to instructors, the career placement center, your academic advisor, and internship coordinators, and call various companies that interest you.

Once you get an internship, make certain to present yourself as a professional. Treat this experience as a real job. Dress appropriately, use effective communication skills, act maturely, show that you're dependable and responsible, and give it a 100 percent effort. You don't want to be treated as a student. You want to be regarded as a co-worker. Your dress, image, and overall appearance will project you as either a serious career professional or a student who is just putting in the time to get credit for an internship.

EXERCISE 2.2   Creative Brainstorming

Cast a wide net and brainstorm from a broad perspective. You have a job objective, but there may be many jobs and companies that could creatively use your talents. Creative problem solving starts by asking questions.

Don't be concerned if you can't immediately pinpoint the exact job or company or even industry that you want. You can narrow your search as you get into the critical-thinking stage. Just keep in mind how important creativity is in researching jobs. You will want to consider size, location, growth potential, training programs, professional level of staff, and so on. There is a hidden job market out there. Look beyond the obvious.

Based on information you've been able to gather from resources up to this point, ask yourself the following questions as you fill in the following worksheet. This exercise will help you eliminate companies or jobs that don't match your tastes and interests, and help you pinpoint potentially interesting job opportunities.

Which companies will help me advance in my field and meet my career goals?

_____

Which companies and jobs are in areas of the country I would like to live in?

_____

Which companies and jobs have good training and education programs?

_____

Which companies and industries are expanding? Which are shrinking?

_____

Which companies are about the right size for me? Would I prefer working in a small or large company?

_____

Which companies seem to share my values (for example, high ethical standards, concern for the environment, quality products, customer service)?

_____

EMPLOYEE EMPOWERMENT

Workplace Trends

Key: Self-Reliance

In the past, employees joined a company and worked their way up the ladder until they retired. In most cases, they enjoyed an income higher than that of their parents. There was a paternal climate assuring workers that if they were loyal and did their jobs well the company would take care of them and they would have lifelong employment. But in today's workplace, security is a thing of the past; change is a part of life. Job security has vanished. Even as the U.S. economy grows, downsizing continues. In 1993, 600,000 jobs were cut.

If you are the average person, you will change jobs or even careers four or five times in your life. Businesses may close or merge, you may be fired or laid off, you may want a new challenge in the same field, or you may want to shift into a whole new job area. You will redefine lifelong employment as a series of jobs at different companies. The successful worker will be prepared for the unexpected.

The prepared worker will take additional classes to learn new technical and human relations skills. The prepared worker will continually build a strong and diverse network of professional contacts. The prepared worker will have a plan of action thought out for the unexpected and will have an answer to the question, What would I do if I were fired tomorrow? The prepared worker will have an updated resumé ready and have polished interviewing skills. The prepared worker will be a take-charge professional who takes personal responsibility for career success.

Career Strategies: Become self-reliant, mobile, prepared, and willing to accept responsibility for your career.

Network for Career Success!

There is no doubt about it: Effective networking produces jobs and is vital for lasting career success. Good jobs are all around you, but most—at least 80 percent—are never listed in the want ads. This "who-do-you-know" method of hiring is common; therefore, the more you talk to people, the better your chances of finding a job in the hidden job market.

Building a community of professional people is your greatest resource for gaining access to jobs, getting referrals, and getting promoted. Networks create the vital link between you and the people who have the authority to hire you. They also provide personal and professional benefits: fulfillment, fellowship, and a sense of real joy. Networking is the best way to communicate your goals, skills, qualifications, and personal qualities to others.

Networking

- Provides contacts with people who can refer you to jobs.
- Connects you with other professionals.
- Serves as a forum for sharing job-search strategies.
- Is an important ongoing career skill.

Networking means talking to and building rapport with qualified people. Networking is relationship building. Networks are the web of people you know from all walks of life. They may not be managers, company presidents, or owners of small businesses, but they know someone who can introduce you to people who do the hiring. Networking builds a resource bank of professionals who can give you support, advice, and encouragement, and it also increases your visibility.

Networking is also an important job skill that will help you do well in your job, help you get promoted, and enhance your personal and professional life.

EXERCISE 2.3 Assess Your Network System

Make a list of people you relate to professionally and people you know personally who may have job contacts. Don't evaluate who could best help you or who you should call. At this time, just concentrate on writing any name that comes to mind. Here's a list of possible network sources:

- Former classmates.
- Members in professional associations.
- Family members and relatives.
- Friends of family members.
- Present colleagues and co-workers.
- Past colleagues and co-workers.
- Present boss or former bosses.
- Customers and previous customers.
- Neighbors.
- The local chamber of commerce staff.
- Newspaper editors and writers of newsletters and journals.
- Community members in clubs or associations to which you belong.
- Members of professional clubs and meetings.
- Placement officials.
- Professional acquaintances who are bankers, stockbrokers, accountants, real estate brokers, insurance agents, elected officials, doctors, dentists, owners of small businesses, instructors, professors, teachers, ministers, fundraising directors, sponsors of the arts, and so on.

Assess your network on a regular basis. You will want to modify your network as your values, experience, and goals change.

My network: Whom do I know?

_____

_____

Supporters

Look at your initial list above and determine who supports you on a daily basis. In the space provided in Exercise 2.4, write down the names of all the people in your life who help you get things done. We'll call these people your supporters. They may be secretaries, student assistants, administrative assistants, clerks, advisors, typists, classmates, friends, family, or support staff. They are at the core of helping you with your work in the job search.

Professionals

In the space provided in Exercise 2.4, write down the names of professionals in related areas or fields who have expertise and whom you respect. If you are a student, these professionals may be counselors, professors, teachers, administrators, and support staff. If you are a salesperson, they might be hotel workers, suppliers, or staff in the main office. If you are a writer, these people might be editors, publishers, or artists. They may also be professional contacts whose services you use and whom you would recommend to others.

Promoters

Other contacts may be people who have already helped you with your career. They help coach and promote your career. They give you advice and encouragement and can help you look at your career direction. If you are a student, these professional experts may be club or academic advisors, instructors, professors, coaches, career counselors, and so on. They may be your good friends, a favorite uncle, a next-door neighbor, a minister, or your family doctor.

If you are in business, these people may be co-workers, chairs of committees, members of professional organizations, customers, clients, sales staff, and colleagues in other organizations. These people are great sources of information and ideas. They help you to question your goals, challenge you to succeed, and promote your career in a variety of ways.

Role Models

Which people who have achieved success in an area you are interested in serve as your role models? List them in the role-model section of Exercise 2.4. Some of these people you may know. Others you may not know personally, but they nevertheless provide inspiration and an example that you would like to follow. These people may be instructors, professors, community leaders, authors, and noted experts in their profession. They may have demonstrated tremendous courage, resilience, creativity, or sheer hard work. Collect stories about successful people you admire. Find out how they became successful.

Mentors

You may have a small number of people who are not only promoters and coaches, but who provide opportunities and concrete guidance on a personal basis. Mentors can be role models, or they can be professionals outside your career area who take an interest in your career. They are generally well-established and successful in their own careers. They make suggestions, inform you of opportunities, introduce you to key people, help you become more visible, and guide your career. They help you set goals, provide you with guidance, and assist you as you face important career decisions. They provide connections to other important people and refer you to essential resources. They are real people in your life whom you respect and want to emulate. List these contacts under mentors in Exercise 2.4.

EXERCISE 2.4   **Defining Your Network**

Supporters	Professionals	Promoters	Role Models	Mentors

Network Strategy #1: Get Organized

It is important to keep your network system organized. Here are a few tips:

- Keep names of contacts in a notebook or on your computer and update your list often.

- When you meet a new contact, ask for a business card or write down the information on a note card. If possible, get the person's home phone number.

- When you have a moment, jot down information about this person on the back of the card—shared interest, ideas, projects he or she is working on, possible opportunities—and put the cards in your record-keeping system (see Chapter 1).

- For all your contacts, set up work sheets like the one at the top of page 49. This allows you to see the growing network you are creating.

Name	Company	Phone	Date Called	Call Back	Result	Other Information
1. Cathy Banes	ABC, Inc.	822-2938	9/1/94	9/2/93	Interview	Sent literature
2.						
3.						
4.						
5.						

Network Strategy #2: Build Your Network

You should now have listed contacts (Exercise 2.2) and organized them into categories (Exercise 2.3). Review your list and see where you need to build contacts. You may discover that you need to go to professional meetings, get more involved in the community, or re-establish contact with old friends and classmates.

Think of fresh ways you can build your network. Use creative problem solving to come up with new contacts. For example, brainstorm ideas with a friend: "Mark, didn't your roommate in college have an uncle in banking?" "Lily, isn't your niece dating someone whose father works for a large computer firm?" "Jan, didn't your brother work for an auto firm in Detroit?"

One effective way to build your network is to contact personal and professional friends and take them out for coffee or lunch. Ask them for other contacts in your field or contacts that they might have in a company you're interested in. Be prepared to invest time, positive feedback, and money in giving back to people something for their time and help. Take people to lunch, send them interesting articles, introduce them to people you think would help their own careers. Remember, the more people who know you want a job, the greater your chances of landing a job you want. Don't assume that even your best friends or co-workers know your skills, past job experiences, accomplishments, or career goals.

The main point to remember is that networking doesn't just happen. Like anything else in life, you must cultivate and nurture your networking contacts if they are to expand and support you. See every contact as a means to gaining information, building professional and personal contacts, and advancing in your career.

High-Tech Networking

Internet and various on-line services can plug you into a network without your actually having to meet professionals in the field. Buy an Internet directory at a bookstore. Just remember, blatant self-marketing is inappropriate using *any* medium.

The most successful job searchers start to network in high school and continue when they go to college. They

- Do an internship.
- Do volunteer work.
- Work part time.
- Help their instructors with projects.
- Get to know students in their classes and exchange phone numbers.
- Join professional organizations.
- Get to know professionals and ask them about their careers.
- Use the guidance of instructors, career counselors, advisors, deans, administrators, and staff to explore options.

Get involved in the field you are really interested in and build your network. For example, if your field is environmental planning, join environmental clubs and volunteer your services to a state or federal agency. If your field is in computers, find a part-time job at a computer store or a campus or high school computer lab, or ask local businesses if you can help set up a computer system or teach staff. If you have a chance to work for a company, don't be afraid to take an entry-level job.

Network Strategy #3: Expand Your Base

You must go beyond the initial contacts you've listed. Many of the people you contact may not know of openings, but may recommend that you see or call someone else. It helps if you have a mutual acquaintance who you can say has referred you. Expand your network by asking all the contacts on your initial list if they can recommend five people you could contact. Ask them for their counterpart at other companies. If you start with 50 names and each one gives you 5 more, you will quickly see the layers of networking building up. Building a strong network is time-consuming, but it is helpful for getting a job and will benefit your career as well.

Network Strategy #4: Write Networking Letters

The purpose of networking letters is to help you build long-term professional and personal contacts, to keep people informed about your career, and to gather information for your file. The main goal of these letters is to build your network to generate job leads.

It is important to let people know you are looking for a job or about to make a career change. Write letters to friends, family, professional acquaintances, business associates, and to people from your contacts lists who may be able to provide information, advice, and referrals. Whenever possible, it is a good idea to turn these letters into telephone calls and face-to-face meetings.

Some sample networking letters appear below:

July 5, 19__

Linda Sanders, Director of Marketing
J.C. Systems Inc.
531 Bay Ave.
Seattle, WA 98772

Dear Linda,

It has been nearly three years since we last talked at the National Conference on Marketing in Santa Fe. You were most helpful in helping me clarify my career goals.

I'm leaving Consumers Programs after three years of increasingly responsible marketing experiences. I have enjoyed my job but very much want to return to Seattle.

Do you know of any employers in the Seattle area that would be interested in my marketing and computer background? Do you have suggestions as to whom I might call for further contacts?

I'll call you next week to discuss any ideas you may have. I very much appreciate your help and support.

Sincerely,

Jay Turner

December 12, 19__

Dear Bob,

Merry Christmas! This should be one of your earliest greetings. Will you be going back to visit your family in Idaho?

I'm writing to ask your support and advice. As I told you in my last letter, I am ready to start thinking about a job change. Can we meet for coffee or dinner at the FAPPS Conference in January? I want to give this next career move some real thought, and I don't want to jump into anything too quickly. You've always given me invaluable support and advice for my career. I think I want to stay in sales, but this may be a good time to launch myself into an entry-level marketing position.

I'm sending you a copy of the speech I gave at a local seminar and an updated copy of my resumé so you can see the kinds of projects I have been involved in this last year.

I look forward to hearing from you soon. Give Mary and the girls my best.

Warm Regards,

Jay

Network Strategy #5: Informational Interviews

Informational interviews are just that, interviews that help you find out more about your career field and about a certain company. Most of these interviews will be the result of referrals. Referrals get your feet in the door and give you a common connection—even if it is several times removed.

In most cases, an informational interview is not a formal interview for a specific job, so don't do a hard sell. Most professionals enjoy taking a few minutes to talk to someone just going into a field and feel flattered you have asked for their advice about career issues.

Prepare a personal approach when you go for an informational interview. Write out a brief script that focuses on your purpose. You don't want to sound canned, but you also don't want to ramble aimlessly and waste people's time. Practice on a tape recorder until you have a relaxed speech that sounds friendly, direct, and professional. The following are sample openers:

Hello, Ms. Whitney. Thank you for taking the time to meet with me. I think I'd like to be in sales someday for a large company, too. I'd like some advice on getting started in this field from someone who has made it.

Hello, Mr. Wells. My name is Sandra Wooley. May I speak with Ms. Whitney?

I have been told by a mutual friend, Joe Nettles, that Ms. Whitney would be an excellent person with whom to discuss a career decision. When could I see her for a short meeting?

Get to your informational interview a few minutes early. This will give you time to relax, and you may find out information about the company or the job. If the secretary is not busy, ask if you may have a copy of the annual report or company publication. Have a list of questions that you might want to ask during an informational interview.

Questions to Consider

- To what trade journals should I subscribe?
- What professional organizations should I join?
- May I have a copy of the latest annual report?
- What are the advantages and disadvantages of this field?
- What community groups would be good to join?
- Who are other top leaders in this field?
- If you had it to do over again, what would you do differently to succeed in this line of work?
- What companies do you think would be best to apply to?
- What specific advice would you give me that would help me advance in my career?
- Can you give me the names of five other people to contact?

Have a list of questions prepared in case the conversation focuses on the company itself and a possible job opportunity.

- What skills and abilities are most important for this field and for the company?
- What are the biggest concerns and problems facing this company?
- What is the corporate culture? (Values, or set of norms)
- Is this a good company in which to learn the field and get promoted?
- What is the company's mission and philosophy of management?
- What are the most common day-to-day problems?
- Does this company encourage training and learning new skills?

Networking Strategy #6: Cold Calling

Cold calling (calling someone you don't know and to whom you haven't been referred) is useful for gaining informational interviews. I suggest you do it, but it does require a positive attitude and the willingness to risk rejection. Since most people would rather help someone who is a friend or at least a friend of a friend, you may encounter some resistance when you call a total stranger. The key to success in cold calling is to be pleasant and to practice. Don't do a hard sell, but ask to discuss the field, your career, or questions you have about the company. When you make calls every day or several times a week, you improve your technique. With persistent effort, you will get interviews. Remember, you control the number of calls you make and your state of mind. Don't take rejection personally. This take-charge attitude will also contribute to your success on your new job.

Sometimes, you will hear of an opening or have an interest in a company or a specific office. You may hear that the center arts program at a college just lost its graphic designer, and you want to explore the possibility of working for them. Go for it! Follow these tips:

Guidelines for cold calling

1. Get as many details about the position as you can from the source.
2. Call the company and find out who the department supervisor is in charge of the department. This is the person with the authority to hire you.
3. Get the person's correct name, spelling, pronunciation, and phone number.
4. Get the person's secretary's name, spelling, pronunciation, and phone number.
5. Call the secretary. The conversation should go something like this:

   Hello Ms. Timmons. My name is Jan Foss. May I speak with Mr. Little, please? The secretary may ask what the call is about. If so, say some thing such as, *This regards a career question. I would like to speak to him this week if possible.* (If he is not available, ask if you can arrange a short meeting at his convenience.)

Notice that you are not asking *if* you can meet with the decision maker, but *when*. Also notice that you did not tell the secretary you are looking for a job. Most secretaries will steer you to the personnel office or protect their boss from people who are trying to get jobs. You are asking for career advice and a chance to show what you can do for the company. Limit the information you are giving out. (Never answer questions that haven't been asked.) Your goal is to either meet with the person who has the authority to hire or to at least engage in a phone conversation. If you don't get a call back, call again in a few days. Be courteous, but persistent.

Don't feel as if you are wasting someone's time by asking for an informational interview. As long as you keep your meetings short and you are respectful, most professionals are flattered that you want to know about the field they are in or that you are interested in working for the company.

EXERCISE 2.5   Write a Cold-Calling Script

Write out a script so you know what you are going to say and what your goals are for the phone conversation. For example, your goals may be to gain information, discuss career options, find out information about the company, or inquire about job openings.

Goals:_____

Phone script:_____

It's incredibly important that you follow up any type of networking meeting. Write a note thanking the person for taking the time to talk with you either by phone or in person. A handwritten note is more personal than a typed letter and shows you have taken the time to be gracious. This is not just good manners; it also serves as one more memory jogger to who you are. Don't send it on office stationery, and use your own stamps. Don't forget the receptionist and/or secretary. She or he often has a lot of influence with the boss. Write a handwritten note showing appreciation for his or her arranging the meeting, the professional manner with which you were treated, the coffee, and so on.

As you build a network, nurture it and follow up with people who have helped you:

- Send articles of interest, holiday cards, and notes of congratulations for an achievement, and make periodic phone calls.
- If you know someone has been laid off or is looking for a job, send a note offering your understanding and help.
- If someone has a concern or is working on a new project, send them related articles or information about how you solved a similar problem.

Network Strategy #7: Alumni Contacts

Once you graduate, use the alumni office to match your interests with alumni who are working in related fields. Then call alumni and introduce yourself. You'll be surprised at the positive response you will get. Even alumni who have graduated years before you will most likely be delighted to talk with you about career planning. Ask for a short interview either by phone or in person, so that you can ask specific questions about job openings and what their job involves. Describe the job you are interested in, the skills you have to offer, and ask for five or six professional contacts. Ask them what professional associations they would suggest you join. Make certain you contact every person recommended and ask that person for five more contacts. Your network will grow, and you will be amazed at how valuable these contacts will be for you over your career. Not only will they open up new opportunities, but you will enrich your professional contacts and build friendships.

Network Strategy #8: Networking through Service

Community service can provide the connection between school and the real world. You can demonstrate that you are an involved person, a problem solver, and a doer. You will stand out from other candidates who may have a degree but whose excuse is that they didn't have time to contribute. The benefits are both personal and professional. You will gain contacts and high visibility (helping expand your network) and learn on-the-job skills. The real benefit, however, is knowing you are giving something back to society. Get involved in the community and campus. There are hundreds of agencies that can use your talents:

Community	Campus
Hospitals	Campus ministry
Nursing homes	Environmental clubs
Homeless shelters	Sports
Schools	Theatre clubs
Nonprofit agencies	Journalism clubs
Red Cross	Multicultural clubs
Cancer Society	Student volunteers
Junior League	Tutoring
Literacy programs	
AIDS support work	
Girl Scouts	
Boy Scouts	
Senior citizen centers	
Animal shelters	

Networkworking Tips

1. Be prepared. Know what you want and have a list of questions. Don't waste other people's time.

2. Be positive. Have a positive attitude and show enthusiasm. No one likes to be around a whiner.

3. Be generous. Send ideas, articles, and names of contacts to others. Share ideas and remember that networking is a two-way process.

4. Be a risk taker. Set goals for networking and build them into your everyday life. Talk with people you don't know at meetings, and introduce yourself at various events. Stretch your comfort level.

5. Be respectful. Be brief and respectful and don't ask for too much. You don't want to appear insensitive or bold.

6. Be trustworthy. Never betray another person's confidentiality or trust. Never gossip.

7. Be a doer. Follow up on leads.

8. Be courteous. Send thank-you notes to people who have given you support, advice, time, and referrals.

Networking is one of the most powerful tools you can use in your job search. Networking is also a valuable job success tool that will pay off throughout your professional career. Networking is a give-and-take process that involves helping others with their careers and building a solid relationship based on mutual respect.

THE BENEFIT FACTOR

The Benefit Factor

The benefit of internships is hard to overstress. It is difficult to find a good job if you don't know what is out there. Networking provides contacts, information, and awareness. Internships, job-training programs, summer jobs, part-time and full-time jobs, and volunteer work can enhance your network, provide contacts, and give you information about new jobs. Going to school full time without networking or being involved in the job world keeps you isolated. Of course, it is important to get an education and a college degree or certificate, but education need not take the place of experience. Get involved in the world of work as soon as you can. Studies indicate that a liberal arts major with internship or job experience in business is more likely to get a business job than a business major without work experience. As a new college or training school graduate, you will stand out if you have some solid experience and exposure to the real world of work.

1. What internships are available?
2. How can you find out more?

HITTING THE WALL

One of the hardest things to do during the job search process is to remember to be persistent and confident when you face rejection. Networking is tough even when people are helpful, but it's particularly difficult when you are rejected. You may run into some people who are rude, curt, or just too busy to give you the time of day. The thought of facing another day of calling people can be overwhelming, especially if you are shy.

Scaling the Wall

Researching companies can also get tedious. It may seem as if you are spending hours in the library, talking on the phone, and pursuing leads. We call this feeling "hitting the wall" because it feels as if you just cannot get beyond this huge barrier. Discouragement sets in, your energy dips, the tide is out, and what remains is the mud flats of low self-esteem and depression.

Scaling the Wall

As in every part of the job-search process, your attitude is critical during the exploring and networking process. Your attitude is more important than any other factor in how people will respond to you.

1. Focus on your successes and keep a list of your achievements. Don't dwell on the negative.
2. Keep things in perspective. Not everyone will return your calls, but you will build your network if you are persistent.
3. Act positive. Some days you will not feel enthusiastic. Put on a smile anyway and stay with your action plan.
4. Develop a reputation for being supportive, kind, tactful, honest, and straightforward.
5. Assess your skills, your personal qualities, and your network, and set goals for improving your attitude.
6. Overcome shyness by focusing on others.
7. Learn from and correct your mistakes, but don't dwell on them.
8. Be a problem solver, not a whiner. Approach your problems as opportunities for growth.
9. A positive attitude is a habit. Create good habits by using positive selftalk every day.
10. Use the power of imagery. See yourself being successful.

The Knockout Factor	The Success Factor
• Only use traditional research methods.	• Explore both traditional and nontraditional methods.
• Don't use creative problem solving.	• Use creative problem solving.
• Fear rejection and act timid.	• Build your confidence and sense of worth.
• Keep your job search to yourself.	• Create a network of professional and personal contacts.
• Give up too soon.	• Be persistent and positive.
• Don't set goals.	• Set goals and daily priorities.
• Don't network.	• Write a script and call someone every day.
• Be disorganized.	• Develop a record-keeping system.

PROBLEM SOLVING AT WORK

Problem Solving

Josh will graduate in a year with a degree in computer technology from a business school in Ohio. He is just starting to plan his job search. He is enjoying the traditional method of researching jobs, and companies and creating a resumé. He has been told that it is who you know that counts when it comes to finding a job. Josh has friends who attend professional conferences, volunteer in the community, set up information meetings with business leaders, and make cold calls to professionals.

Josh's problem is that he is shy and doesn't feel he has the confidence, personality, or skill to explore nontraditional job-search methods. Should Josh stick with the traditional methods of job hunting or explore nontraditional methods as well?

Use the problem-solving guide below to give you direction. (On the next page you'll see the result of Josh's networking.)

1. Have I clearly stated the problems? Should I use traditional, nontraditional, or a combination of both methods of job searching?

2. Do I have enough information? Do I have all the information I need to make a decision? Have I researched the benefits of networking and internships?

3. Can I make the decision by myself? What resources are available to help me make a better decision? Have I talked with a career counselor, my advisor, or my instructors?

4. Have I brainstormed alternatives? What other methods are available? Could I start by talking with friends and family rather than jumping right into cold calling?

5. Have I looked at likely consequences? If I begin to build an active networking base, will I increase my chances of getting a job? What other consequences might occur if I have a strong network?

6. Have I identified all the resources and tools needed? Have I researched the resources available? Am I aware of the existence of Toastmasters (a public speaking club) and speech classes, which could help me overcome my shyness and develop better communication skills? Am I willing to acquire the additional skills and tools to be successful?

7. Have I developed and implemented an action plan? Have I designed an action plan that will help me make sound decisions?

8. Have I identified the best solution and done everything possible to ensure success? Have I made a decision using critical thinking and creativity? Am I committed to making the decision a success?

9. Have I assessed the results? Have I evaluated my decision to see if it is working? Have I assessed my grades, work satisfaction, and goals?

10. Have I modified the plan, if necessary? What adjustments could I make that would make my decision more successful?

How Networking Produces Results

Josh decided to call his good friend, Adam, who attended West Technical College in Massachusetts and worked one summer as an intern in the alumni affairs office. Josh asked Adam if he knew anyone in the computer business in the Boston area. Adam referred him to Joe and Anne Springer. Joe is the director of alumni at West Tech Business College, and Anne is the director of software at Compco Computer Company. After several phone calls, Josh talked directly to Joe. Joe referred him to Anne. Anne gave Josh several contacts and told him to keep her posted. Josh was assertive and persistent and worked at his job search full time. He called all the contacts, asked questions, and listened. They gave him more contacts, which he developed into an impressive list. In just a few short weeks, Josh had an incredible network of professional contacts in the Boston area.

He also used traditional sources for finding jobs. In fact, the lead that resulted in his final job offer came from an ad. But it was the networking that helped him finalize the job he wanted. Josh was not only rewarded for his persistent, hard work by landing a job, but he has the beginning of a professional network that will result in many lifelong professional associations. Once he accepted the job, Josh sent out a note to everyone on his network list.

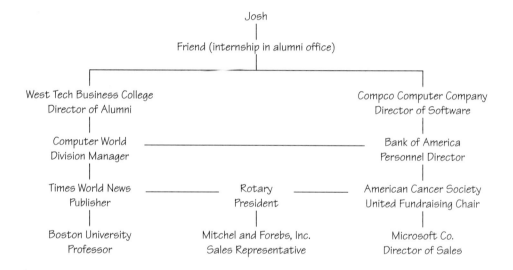

Research and Networking Strategies

- Set immediate and long-term goals and daily priorities.
- Explore both traditional and nontraditional job-search methods.
- Assess your network.
- Use creative problem solving and critical thinking.
- Build your network.
- Expand your base.
- Write network letters.
- Conduct informational interviews.
- Follow up.
- Be positive and persistent.
- Create internships.
- Explore alumni contacts.

Chapter Checklist   Yes   No

1. Have you set goals and priorities?
2. Have you written a specific action plan?
3. Have you explored job options using
   - Traditional methods?
   - Nontraditional methods?
   - Creative problem solving?
   - Critical thinking for decision making?
4. Have you assessed and expanded your network?
5. Have you set goals and set up informational interviews?
6. Have you explored internships?
7. Have you kept in touch with your network?

Resumés

Introduction

The resumé is a critical tool to help you get your foot in the door. In this chapter, we will look at the overall image and specific factors involved in writing an effective resumé. You will also get practical advice and practice translating your skills into specific benefits for a company.

Now that your strategic planning is done, you can organize that information into a resumé that stands out and really says who you are. Your autobiography and the self-assessment exercises in Chapters 1 and 2 will pay off now. In these exercises, you've begun to discover what you have to offer. Now you can begin showing connections between your strengths, accomplishments, and skills and the needs of a company or your targeted employer.

First impressions really do count. Often your resumé is the first contact the employer will have with you. Your resumé can make or break you. You want your resumé to stand out, look professional, and highlight your skills. The resumé should

- Demonstrate that you are capable of performing the job you are applying for.
- Highlight your education and skills.
- Highlight your accomplishments.
- Show a connection between your skills and how they have benefited other companies.

Learning Objectives

In Chapter 3, you will learn

- The essential factors of a good resumé.

- How to write a job objective.

- How to highlight your experience.

- How to choose the best resumé format.

- How to use action words.

- How to focus on the benefit factor.

There is a lot of controversy about how effective a resumé really is at helping you land a job. The purpose of a resumé is to get you an invitation to an interview. It is the *interview* that will get you the job, not the resumé. Resumés are often used to screen out applicants, so you want your resumé to stand out, be easy to read, be general enough to reach a large market, and be specific enough to clearly indicate your skills. The resumé is important for many other reasons:

1. Self-assessment. Writing a resumé requires a process of self-assessment that sets the tone and the foundation for the entire job-search process. It defines your skills, accomplishments, and experiences as they relate to a job and helps you to bring your job objective into focus.

2. Standard policy. Many companies have standard hiring procedures that require a resumé when you apply for a position. Even if the company knows you well, a resumé may be required "for the file."

3. Interview questions. In most cases, you will be asked to send or bring your resumé, even if you're invited personally to meet with the employer. The interviewer will scan your resumé and ask questions about your past performance based upon your experience, skills, and qualifications. You must be able to explain and elaborate on your resumé at the interview.

4. Memory jogger. A resumé can serve as a reminder or memory jogger to the employer after you have been interviewed. This is perhaps one of the most important aspects of the resumé.

5. A reflection of you. The resumé is not only a reflection of your skills and experience, but of your style, sense of organization, and neatness.

6. Increase your chances. Although personal contact is always preferred over a piece of paper or a phone interview, direct contact with the hiring authority is not always possible. By sending your basic resumé and specific cover letter to many companies, you may increase your chances of getting the job you want.

You can see that a resumé is an important and necessary tool in the job-search process. Job-search strategies are all tools that complement each other and work together. It bears repeating: A resumé is not only a summary of your skills, experience, and education, it also reflects who you are and what you can do. In order to be effective, a resumé must stand out.

Definite vs. Maybe

Most employers are busy and don't take the time to read the vast number of resumés they receive. They skim through them, reading a few lines and put them into piles. They toss out those that are not right for the job, those that lack the necessary education or training, and those that are messy or have misspelled words. There is a pile of "maybes" and a pile of "definite interest." Those in the definite interest pile get a closer look and are invited to come for an interview. You want your resumé to be in the definite interest pile, and you want to be invited for an interview. Nothing happens until you meet face-to-face with the employer. A good resumé will get you the interview.

The effective resumé is designed to highlight your experience, education, skills, interests, and talents in a clear, organized manner. It represents you and must therefore sell you. Remember, you are selling yourself, not your degree, major in school, or present job title. Therefore, your resumé needs to be planned, organized, and polished to reflect your unique accomplishments and skills.

Essential Pieces of an Effective Resumé

The key to an effective resumé is to organize the information about your experience and skills in a clear, concise, easy-to-read, and appealing manner. The following is an example of a resumé that will get read. (The numbers in the left margin are for the sake of discussion and should not appear on the resumé.)

KATIE J. JENSEN

1. **Present address**   **Permanent address**
1423 10th Street   812 La Jolla Avenue
Arlin, Minnesota 52561   Burlingate, Wisconsin 53791
(313) 724–2896   (401) 792–1928

2. **JOB OBJECTIVE:** To obtain an entry-level job as a travel agent.

3. **EDUCATION**
Arlin Community College, Arlin, Minnesota
Associate of Arts in Business, June 1994
  Magna Cum Laude graduate
Cross Pointe Career School, Arlin, Minnesota
  Certificate in Tourism, June 1992

4. **HONORS AND AWARDS**
Academic Dean's list
Recipient of Burlingate Rotary Scholarship, 1992

5. **WORK EXPERIENCE**
UNIVERSITY TRAVEL AGENCY, Arlin, Minnesota
Tour Guide, August 1993–present
• Arrange tours to historic sites in a four-state area. Responsibilities include contacting rail and bus carriers, arranging for local guides at each site, making hotel and restaurant reservations, and providing historical information about points of interest.
• Develop tours for holidays and special events. Responsibilities include pre-event planning, ticketing, and coordination of travel and event schedules.
• Specialized tour planning resulted in 24 percent increase in tour revenues over the preceding year.

BURLINGATE AREA CONVENTION CENTER, Burlingate, Minnesota
Intern Tourist Coordinator, December 1992–June 1993
• Established initial contact with prospective speakers, coordinated schedules, and finalized all arrangements. Set up computerized database of tours using dBase 1V.
• Organized receptions for groups up to 250, including reserving meeting rooms, contacting caterers, finalizing menus, and preparing seating charts.

6. **CAMPUS AND COMMUNITY ACTIVITIES**
• Vice President Tourist Club, 1993–1994.
• Co-chaired 1992 Home-tour fundraising event for Big Sisters.

7. **PROFESSIONAL MEMBERSHIP**
• Burlingate Area Convention and Visitors Bureau

A separate reference list should also be available, like the one below.

KATIE J. JENSEN

References

Ms. Jan A. Tostee
Instructor of Business
Cross Pointe Career School
Arlin, Minnesota 49002
(313) 724–1728

Mr. John D. Rogers
Instructor of Business
Arlin Community College
Arlin, Minnesota 49003
(313) 724–8924

Mr. Thomas Jones
Supervisor
University Travel Agency
Arlin, Minnesota 49002
(313) 726–3845

Ms. Janice Hines
Co-worker, sales
Burlingate Area Convention Center
Burlingate, Wisconsin 53702
(401) 792–5423

Now that you have filled out the personal inventory in the database exercise in Chapter 1; have reflected on your strengths, achievements, and skills; and have researched companies, you have taken the first steps to writing an effective resumé. Your investment in self-assessment will add focus and clarity to your resumé. Take the information in your database inventory and organize it into the basic sections.

A letter-perfect resumé is an easy-to-read presentation of your skills, experiences, and accomplishments. You will want to choose the format and style that best reflects your experiences and background.

Guidelines for a Letter-Perfect Resumé

1. Keep resumé to one page for an entry-level job.
2. Focus on skills and achievements.
3. Use action words to define duties.
4. Keep it formal and businesslike.
5. Make certain it is grammatically correct and free of errors.
6. Keep it clear, concise, and easy to read.
7. Present data in reverse chronological order (most recent first).
8. Print on good quality paper.
9. Make certain all information is correct and verifiable.

Resumé Categories

1. Identification

Write your name, address, and telephone number. Don't use a nickname. If you have a temporary or school address and phone, you will want to include a permanent address and phone number as well. Don't include other personal information (marital status, height, weight, health, travel, interests, hobbies) unless you think it is relevant to the job or will increase your chances of getting the job. Never include a picture of yourself. Adding gimmicks or fluff only detracts from the essential information and clutters up your resumé. Keep information to the essentials. However, if you decide your hobbies are relevant to your job objective or indicate an important skill or personal quality, put them at the end of the resumé or on a separate sheet of paper that you can take with you to the interview.

(one inch from top)

ROBERT L. LEWIS
378 Park Lane
Lake Pleasant, Michigan 48092
(810) 724–1876

2. Job objective: Plus or Minus?

It is not essential that you include a job objective on your resumé. The rule of thumb is to include a job objective if you will *only* accept a specific job. The rationale is that you don't want to limit yourself. Most new graduates want to gain experience and will accept various jobs in a company. For example, you may really want to be an editor with a publishing company, but the company may want you to work in field marketing or sales so you that you will gain valuable experience and get to know the service area. If you state your job objective as an editor on your resumé, you may not get called back even if the company is impressed with your skills and abilities and has openings in sales.

Instead of writing a specific job objective on your resumé, you can use the cover letter to relate your resumé to the specific job you are applying for. You will see examples of how to relate your job objective clearly in Chapter 4.

However, if you want to use a job objective on your resumé and you have a printer, you can change the job objective for each resumé that you send out. By completing the exercises in Chapters 1 and 2, you have begun to get an idea of what is important to you in a job, what you do well, and what you like to do. You have researched jobs in order to relate your skills and interests to the type of work that best suits you. Your goal now is to define a job objective—a specific statement of the type of job for which you would like to apply. If you are having trouble writing a job description, review resources listed in Chapter 2, such as the *Occupational Outlook Handbook* or review your networking contacts for people who work in the field you are interested in exploring.

Write a specific job objective if you have a specific job target, such as a dental assistant. Keep it general if you are willing to accept different jobs, such as an entry-level position in sales, marketing, or management. Complete this exercise even if you have decided not to include a job objective on your resumé. Once you have targeted your job objective, you will add more direction to your job search.

JOB OBJECTIVE
(specific)
To obtain an entry-level position as an occupational therapist.

(general, but not too broad)
To obtain an entry-level position in business administration that will utilize my computer, organizational, and accounting skills.

What kind of job do you want?

_____

_____

_____

Write your own job objective:

_____

_____

_____

3. Education

List your education in reverse chronological order (most recent degree first). Spell out the degree in full.

List school, city and state, your degree or certificate, major, date of graduation, and GPA (if over 3.0).

EDUCATION

Michigan State University, East Lansing, Michigan
Bachelor of Science in Mechanical Engineering, 1996

Lake Harbor Community College, Lake Harbor, Ohio
Associate Degree in Business, 1994
Major: Accounting
GPA: 3.6

Some formats list date, school, location, degree, and GPA:

1994   SAN JOSE CAREER COLLEGE   San Jose, CA
      Bachelor of Arts in Business   GPA 3.5

If you have a college or career school degree or certificate, don't list your high school. If you are still in college or career school, you can list your high school if you choose:

Bennett Career School, Burlingate, Wisconsin
Associate of Science in Respiratory Therapy
Expected date of graduation   June 1995

La Jolla High School, Burlingate, Wisconsin
High School Diploma   June 1993

List your minor area of study, specific courses, workshops, seminars, or training programs if you think they are relevant and will help you get the job. Otherwise, keep your education section brief. You can expand on your education in your cover letter, application, or in the interview, by specifying how certain courses relate to a specific job

Certification, Licensure, or Advanced Training

Under "Education," list certificates and licenses you have earned, as well as any advanced training you have received. For consistency, follow the same format for dates.

CERTIFICATION
1994   Certificate in Food Management and Sanitation
1992   Certificate in CPR

LICENSURE
Registered Emergency Medical Technician, 1993
Rehabilitation License in Nursing for the State of Wyoming, 1992

1994   E.C.C. Radiotelephone Third-Class Operator License

University of Illinois, Chicago, Illinois
Continuing Education Management Series, June 1994–1995

4. Honors and Awards

If you received college honors or a fellowship, you will want to list these as part of your education regardless of how long you have been out of school. This is also an appropriate place to indicate that you have paid for a significant portion of your education.

HONORS AND AWARDS

- Academic Dean's list
- National Honor Society

EXERCISE 3.2   Education and Honors

Write out all your educational experiences, certificates, honors, and awards.

_____

_____

_____

_____

_____

5. *Work Experience*

List your work experience in reverse chronological order (starting with your most recent job).

- List the dates (year is sufficient).
- List the name and location (city and state) of the company.
- List your job title.
- Describe your duties and responsibilities.
- Don't forget internships, apprenticeships, on-the-job training programs, part-time and summer job experiences that relate to the job you are applying for.

EXPERIENCE

1993–present   ADAMS ELECTRIC COMPANY   Seashore, FL
Electrician

- Calculated plans in compliance with latest N.C. codes and regulations.
- Implemented plans for wiring diagrams.

or use this order:

Tour Guide   GLOBETRAVEL   Englewood, New Jersey
August 1995–present

- Coordinated tours to historic sites.
- Developed new holiday tour package. Resulted in 24 percent increase in revenues.

Job Descriptions

List three or four key duties under your most recent job and two or three for previous jobs. For many people, this is a difficult part of writing the resumé. Review your job duties and choose action verbs and short statements to describe them. Don't use complete sentences. Whenever possible, be clear about how you have benefited the company. Here are several examples:

- Created automated accounting system. Resulted in 40 percent cost savings.
- Developed sales promotions, negotiated and wrote sales contracts. Increased revenue by 33 percent during first year.
- Provided customer service to store patrons.
- Responsible for window displays. Won 1993 Creative Advertisement Award.
- Revised reporting procedures to comply with government regulations.
- Provided administrative services for department.

- Supervised a staff of six volunteers.
- Drafted reports and edited papers and articles.
- Collaborated with clinicians on proper treatment.
- Coordinated activities and prepared daily reports.

Action Verbs

The personality and team-style exercise in Chapter 1 helped you determine your dominant style. This exercise can also help you choose action words to use in the experience section of your resumé. Review your dominant style and choose the action words that best highlight your style, indicate your diversity, and are most appropriate in relation to the job you are applying for. Add to this list:

Director	Creator	Thinker	Relator
Persuaded	Created	Compiled	Adapted
Administered	Designed	Calculated	Served
Organized	Coached	Analyzed	Cared for
Negotiated	Visualized	Set criteria	Teamed with
Ordered	Attracted	Evaluated	Supported
Controlled	Invented	Formulated	Communicated
Carried out	Demonstrated	Reviewed	Balanced
Developed	Engaged	Regulated	Coordinated
Established	Entertained	Monitored	Assisted

Here is a list of general action words to use for appropriate jobs and activities:

Other Action Words

Acted	Cared for	Demonstrated	Guided
Adjusted	Clarified	Designed	Illustrated
Administered	Coached	Directed	Implemented
Analyzed	Communicated	Discovered	Increased
Applied	Completed		Instructed
Appraised	Conducted	Edited	Integrated
Arranged	Constructed	Enforced	
Assembled	Consulted	Evaluated	Justified
Assisted	Controlled		
	Coordinated	Facilitated	Kept
Balanced	Created	Formulated	Keynoted
Built			
Briefed	Delegated	Generated	

Led	Organized	Reorganized	Supervised
Licensed		Repaired	Supported
	Participated in	Reported	Surveyed
Maintained	Performed	Researched	
Managed	Planned		Taught
Mediated	Prepared	Scheduled	Teamed with
Monitored	Promoted	Screened	Trained
Motivated	Proposed	Selected	
	Provided	Served	Updated
Negotiated	Published	Simplified	
		Solved	Wrote
Operated	Reduced	Structured	

Nouns

Many companies are now using computers to search resumés and store the data for later review. Job computers scan resumés for key words that define the requirements of a particular position. Therefore, you not only need to include action verbs such as those listed above, but also key words for specific occupations. For example, key words for the medical field may include *referral, rehabilitation, treatment,* and *patient care.* Make certain you are familiar with key words in your field and use them when appropriate in your resumé, cover letter, application, and interview.

Skills

Think through the skills you want to demonstrate on your resumé. Here are just a few:

Administrative	Fiscal	Organizational
Artistic	Foreign language	Perceptive
Clerical	Human relations	Persuasive
Communications	Innovative	Planning
Conflict resolution	Inspiring	Presentation
Coordinating	Interpersonal	Problem solving
Counseling	Investigating	Public relations
Critical thinking	Leadership	Public speaking
Debating	Listening	Sales
Decision making	Managerial	Social
Delegation	Mathematical	Supervisory
Design	Mechanical	Team building
Diplomacy	Motivational	Training
Editing	Musical	Working with people
Evaluation	Negotiation	Writing

Use action words for translating your experiences and showing a benefit, as shown in the example below.

Customer Service Representative
Updated ordering system, established new accounts, trained new employees, assisted with marketing plan. Contracted new wholesalers (increased new contacts by 23 percent).

_____

_____

_____

_____

_____

_____

_____

_____

_____

_____

_____

_____

_____

_____

_____

_____

_____

_____

_____

_____

_____

_____

_____

_____

Military Service

Your military experience will fit into the section under work experience. Include the following:

- Branch of service or reserve status.
- Present rank or rank at discharge or position.
- Duties if applicable.
- Dates in the military.
- Honors or achievements.

If you have military experience, make it work for you by translating your duties and achievements into benefits to the company. In Chapter 1, you were asked to assess the value of your military experience. Focus now on the skills you learned, the services you performed, and your benefit to the military. Translate your duties and skills into the ability to follow orders and work as part of a team. Use civilian terms instead of code military words or jargon whenever possible. For example:

Jargon	Civilian term
commanded	directed
soldiers	staff
fighting men	highly trained personnel
long-range patrols	logistic planning

Look at all your duties and responsibilities. Did you lead field teams, make sound decisions, work effectively as a team member, gather and analyze information, maintain equipment, follow through on difficult assignments, and solve problems under stressful conditions? These are all experiences and qualities that any company is interested in. Keep this section brief in your resumé. You can elaborate in the interview when appropriate or on the application form.

MILITARY SERVICE

1992–95   U.S. Army
X-ray specialist (91P). Operated x-ray equipment, assisted radiologist, conducted radiographs, and worked as effective team member.

6. Campus and Community Activities and Service

Campus activities and community service and volunteer experiences are important and can indicate leadership abilities and a willingness to make a contribution. Use action words to describe your duties. (If you have been out of college for several years, don't list campus activities; instead, focus on community involvement.) Include the following:

- Dates.
- Name of community or campus organizations or clubs.
- Position held or duties and responsibilities.

CAMPUS AND COMMUNITY SERVICE

1995   President of Marketing Club.

1994   Co-chaired fundraising event for American Cancer Society (largest profit in event's history).

1992   Youth Educational Services (worked on team to develop statewide grant).

7. Professional Memberships and Activities

List professional memberships, affiliations, and activities. (It is never too early to join professional associations. Most have student discounts, and the professional contacts and job leads are worth the time and expense.) This is also the place to list speeches you have given or research projects connected with your profession. Dates can be listed in the left margin or after the project.

PROFESSIONAL MEMBERSHIPS AND ACTIVITIES

1994–present   Board Member, American Marketing Association (student liaison with university).

1993–95   Membership, American Society of Marketing.

1995   Presenter, American Occupational Therapist Association, "Using Play Therapy for Children with Learning Disabilities," Washington Medical Center, Washington, D.C.

   Research, "Study Skills of Undeclared Students." Research project for Teaching Institute. Evergreen College, January 1995.

EXERCISE 3.4   The Extras

List campus and community service, professional memberships and activities, and use action words to translate skills. For example:

President of marketing club. Demonstrated leadership and good communication skills. Organized a team for fundraising, increased sales of coffee stand by 25 percent in one year.

_____

_____

References

Like every other aspect of the job-search process, compiling a list of references takes research, planning, rapport with ex-employers and workers, and follow-up. Although some employers might not check references, you must be prepared and have them ready. Never write at the bottom of your resumé, "References available upon request." Always have available a separate page of three to six references. Do not send these unless requested. You don't want the interviewer to call your references until you have had an interview. Type your name in caps and bold at the top of the page.

These references should be professionals who know your work, skills, and personal qualities and who will give you a good recommendation. A supervisor, former boss, co-worker and community contacts (Rotary president, mayor, owner of hardware business) are good choices. Review your networking contacts in Chapter 2 for ideas for references. Always ask permission to use their names, addresses, and phone numbers, and ask what phone number they would like to use or if you can include both work and home phone.

Make certain that the people you ask to be references can give you a good recommendation. Ask directly if they will give you a positive recommendation, and assure them that you will send them a resumé so they can answer questions more knowledgeably.

It is vital that you have a letter of reference from your former supervisor if it's requested. If you left the last position with resentment, or if your relationship with your current boss is cool, you need to mend those fences. The only way to handle this situation is for you to take control. Change your perception of the situation and realize that most former bosses want you to find another job.

First, write a draft of a reference letter to your supervisor and request that he or she edit it, discuss it with you, and send you a final copy on company stationary. If you are still employed at the company, you can ask for your supervisor's support. Even if you are terminated, your former supervisor can be convinced to write you a letter of support if you attempt to mend the fence and assume at least part of the blame for your termination.

The following is a sample draft of a reference letter that you might provide:

> 2930 Apple Lane
> Tulip, Florida 21192
>
>
> May 22, 19__
>
>
> Ms. Jan Tempis, Personnel Director
> Avil Corporation
> Orlando, Florida 28821
>
> Dear Ms. Tempis:
>
> I would like to recommend Jill Burton for an administrative assistant position in your organization.
>
> Jill demonstrated excellent management skills in her position as Human Resource Technician. She is dependable, knowledgeable, and organized. She was responsible for developing a new reference file, organizing marketing lists, and handling all seminar registration details.
>
> Unfortunately, because of restructuring at Sona Company, our new management system required a management trainer with a stronger background and a college degree in management. Ms. Burton is a highly trained professional. I would recommend her for the new position she seeks with your firm.
>
>
> Sincerely,
>
>
> Mark Platton
> Sales Director

If you can get a letter of reference from your boss's boss, that would be a big plus, or you can include one from a former supervisor. Then get two or three references from co-workers, professional colleagues, a past professor, teacher, or community leader.

A TECHNOLOGICAL REVOLUTION

Workplace Trends

Key: Technology
The typical image of the white male corporate manager in a tie and suit and the employee working with his hands is being replaced by a new workforce that blurs the lines between blue and white collar categories. There has been a dramatic rise in technicians—men and women who may wear suits and are considered professionals, but who also work with their hands. According to *CPC's Salary Survey,* September 1989 report, of every 100 job offers manu-facturers made, 79 were to technical graduates.

Computers and other high-tech industries will increase the demand for technicians. According to the Bureau of Labor Statistics, there will be a 37 percent increase in technicians in the years from 1990–2005. These techni-cians will operate computers, repair electronic equipment, run laboratory tests in biotechnology companies, work with patients in hospitals and home health care, and research legal cases and statutes. Technology will be a key both in getting and keeping a job. Many more entry-level jobs will require a working knowledge of computers and office machines. For example, for an entry-level position in telemarketing, you will need to be keyboard conversant on a computer in addition to having good communication skills.
Career Strategies: Learn math and technical skills. Keep current with new technology.

Other Factors in Writing a Perfect Resumé

Now that you have listed essential information and used action words to translate experience into accomplishments, you will want to make certain that your resumé is visually attractive and easy to read. Follow the guidelines below:

Length

Resumés should be clear and concise. Unless you have years of experience, keep your resumé to one page. Focus on the essentials: experience, skills, and accom-plishments. Do not state salary requirements, indicate why you left previous jobs, or indicate a restriction about where you are willing to work. Avoid putting anything on your resumé that might rule you out of an interview. Employers are not impressed when they see a two- or three-page resumé that has a lot of fluff. Your cover letter can highlight certain accomplishments and skills and how they relate to a specific job. During the interview you can elaborate on duties, explain dates, give examples, and go into detail.

Format

There are two basic resumé formats: chronological and functional. All other alternatives, such as combination, creative, organizational, marketing letter, or targeted, are simply variations and are generally not as effective. Examples of all types are shown in this chapter and the chapter appendix. Remember, the purpose of a resumé is to make a good first impression and get you an interview. You do this by presenting yourself in a direct, clear, concise, and honest manner, not by creating illusions, using disguises or gimmicks, or by developing a long, detailed, rambling resumé.

Chronological Resumé

The chronological resumé (like the two shown on pages 79 and 80) puts your most recent experience first and is often recommended as the most effective for stating your experience, education, and skills in a direct and traditional manner. Most traditional employers, such as schools, government, and corporations, want to quickly see experience and education listed in a chronological format. They don't want long detailed paragraphs explaining exactly what job tasks you performed. Nor do they want a list of experiences and jobs that lacks dates.

Use a chronological resumé:

- If you are a recent college graduate, have advanced degrees and/or specialized training, and want to emphasize your education.
- If you want to show career progression.
- If you have not changed jobs frequently.
- If you are still in the same field.

Functional Resumé

Use a functional resumé (like the two shown on pages 81 and 82) when you want to highlight skills, abilities, and qualifications rather than education or specific dates of work experience. A homemaker may want to use a functional resumé when she or he has had years of volunteering keeping the family budget, paying taxes, traveling, and organizing events, but limited formal work experience or education. If you have been out of the job market for a number of years, you will want to organize your accomplishments around the major functions you have performed, such as fundraising, organization, and/or public relations. Highlight the skills that will make you stand out.

Use a functional resumé

- If you have little education but years of experience in the job market, and you want to emphasize experience and skills.
- If your work experience doesn't support your job objective.
- If you are changing occupations.
- If you want to point out specific accomplishments and skills.
- If you have had a variety of job experiences.
- If you are re-entering the job market.

JASON STOOB

Present Address
1332 Palm Street
Amber, Ohio 577
(313) 273–1928

Permanent Address
21 Pleasant Lane
21 Walnut Grove, Ohio 56343
(313) 822–3283

WORK EXPERIENCE

1992–present **Assistant Manager**
Greenview Apartments, Amber, Ohio
• Assisted with maintenance of property.
• Collected rent.
• Resolved conflicts.
• Interviewed new renters.
• Reduced turnover rate by 5 percent.

1991–92 **Salesperson**
Johnson's Men's Store, Amber, Ohio
• Installed software package to improve efficiency of cashier
• Designed publicity for spring show

1991 **Intern Salesperson**
Selters Real Estate Office, Amber, Ohio
• Assisted with the installation of a new computer office system, answered phones, assisted customers, typed contracts, filed loan applications.
• Organized seminars, two home tours.

EDUCATION

1993 Simpson Business College   Amber, Ohio
Associate of Science in Business Administration
Major: Real Estate
Minor: Finance

AWARDS, MEMBERSHIPS AND ACTIVITIES

1992–93 President, Marketing Club
• Served as chair for Faculty Awards Committee for spring banquet.
• Gave tours to prospective business students.
1992 Outstanding Business Student Award
1992 United Way volunteer

Gretchen Cash
1883 8th Street
Tacoma, Washington 93021
(661) 751–2738

EDUCATION:

June 1995	Sequoia Business College	Tacoma, WA

Bachelor of Arts
Major: Business Administration
GPA: 3.6

June 1993	Tacoma Business School	Tacoma, WA

Associate of Arts, Computer Science
Graduated with honors

ADDITIONAL TRAINING:

Communication seminar, Universal Seminars
Financial planning, Tacoma Business School
Computer workshop, Washington State University
Editing and writing workshop, Washington State
  University

SPECIAL QUALIFICATIONS:

- Fluent in Spanish
- Advanced skills in IBM and Apple Computers
- Editing and writing skills

WORK EXPERIENCE

1995 **Management Trainee**
ROCKWAY CORPORATION, Tacoma, WA
- Developed computer-based system for customer service.
- Assisted with staff development program.
- Planned and edited newsletter.

1993–95 **Office Manager**
ALLSTATE INSURANCE AGENCY, Tacoma, WA
- Answered the phone, assisted in process claims, maintained files.
- Greeted public, assisted with budget, typed and edited letters.
- Worked with team to develop seminars.
- Improved customer service and company grew over 15 percent in one year.

Venessa Johnson
2988 Pine Avenue
Fair Oaks, Texas 69441
(404) 720–2738

QUALIFICATION AND ACCOMPLISHMENTS

Organizational Skills:

- Demonstrated ability to organize office information system.
- Accurate and detailed bookkeeping inventory.
- Organized fundraiser for American Cancer Society (raised $100,000 for Hospice Center).

Computer Skills:

- Proven ability to learn new software systems quickly.
- Created computer system for payroll for Sunset Elementary School.
- Trained teachers and staff in computer and word processing skills.

Communication Skills:

- Excellent communication with teachers, staff, and parents.
- Created a newsletter for parents and staff.
- Drafted effective business correspondence.

WORK EXPERIENCE

1984–1988   **Secretary,** Sunset Elementary School, Fair Oaks, Texas
1979–84   **Caregiver,** Rainbow Preschool (self-employed), Fair Oaks, Texas

EDUCATION AND TRAINING

Adult Career Training Center, Fairfield, Texas,
Secretarial Certificate, 1990

HONORS AND MEMBERSHIPS

Graduated with Honors
Outstanding Secretarial Student Award

Community Service

Volunteer, American Cancer Society

Robert L. Ferro
613 Park Avenue
Wales, New York 10992
(914) 621–9882

PHOTOGRAPHY

- Designed setups for and photographed interior displays.
- Extensive experience in nature close-ups.
- Taught basic photography to staff.
- Photographed "how-to" series on gardening.
- Illustrated articles on home and garden.
- Supervised photos, illustrations, and drawings.

GRAPHIC DESIGN

- Designed brochures, business cards, newsletters.
- Produced paste-ups for weekly magazine.
- Planned displays for major metropolitan art show.
- Produced flyer for SUNY Art Department.
- Various outdoor journals.

EDITING

- Home show trade magazine.
- *Home and Garden Journal.*
- Articles on interior design.
- Videos for college recruiting.

AWARDS

Home and Garden Magazine Creative Photography Award

EXPERIENCE

1992–present **Free-lance Photographer,** Wales, NY
1991–92   **Graphics Designer and Assistant Editor,** Baltimore, MD
1990–91   **Intern Staff Photographer,** Baltimore, MD

EDUCATION

1991 Maryland Institute of Art, Baltimore, MD
Bachelor of Arts in Commercial and Graphic Arts

Writing Style

The writing style for your resumé should be professional and formal. Be concise, direct, and clear. Use short statements, action words, and bullets to emphasize skills, accomplishments, and duties. Don't use complete sentences, paragraphs, or the word "I." For example, write

- Increased sales by $80,000 in first year.

rather than:

- I worked very hard in sales, visited outlying areas, and increased the sales in my area by $80,000 in 1993.

State your accomplishments directly and clearly. You want to show confidence. However, you must be absolutely truthful and honest. You can be fired for misrepresentation even years after you've been on a job. All information should be verifiable.

Make certain your writing is error free. Check punctuation, grammar, and spelling. Use not only a spell-check, but have a trusted friend or instructor proofread it.

Graphics and Reproduction

Make certain your resumé is visually attractive and professional. Use white space to add balance. Make certain that your resumé is centered.

Don't try to be clever or cute. Unless you are applying to a creative company for a very creative position, use the standard, conservative style for printing and sending your resumé. Use neutral-colored paper, and mail or hand carry it to the company. One person sent his resumé in a shoe with a note that said, "I just want to get my foot in the door." Some companies may appreciate this unusual approach, but in general, you want your basic resumé to be acceptable to many different companies. Save your creative flair for the interview or your first creative assignment.

The general rule is: Keep it simple. Use the following guidelines:

- Avoid graphics and pictures.
- Use basic, nondecorative typefaces.
- Use a standard font size of 10–12 points.
- Avoid script text; use boldface or underline to highlight.
- Avoid too many horizontal and vertical lines.
- Use good quality paper.
- Use classic colors: off-white, cream, beige, or grey.
- Avoid staples or folds.

TAILOR YOUR RESUMÉ

There are services that will prepare a resumé for you; however, it will look like many other candidates' resumés. Write your own resumé. By practicing, you will gain the confidence to write a resumé that reflects you. You will then be able to create different versions to use for a variety of jobs and tailor each one to a specific employer.

There are few hard and fast rules in resumé writing. Try out formats, types, boldface, underlining, and left or right justifications. Choose the combination that best highlights and emphasizes your accomplishments, skills, or expertise and that best fits with your job objective and personal style. I tend to favor clear, concise, and traditional resumés. However, if the standard guidelines and formats seem too conventional and limiting, create your own style and vary your format for different jobs.

EXERCISE 3.6   Putting It All Together

Practice putting together a chronological resumé, using your worksheets as a guide. Compare it with the sample chronological resumé on page 80. Practice writing a functional resumé if you think this format best reflects your skills and accomplishments. See page 82 for a good model.

EXERCISE 3.7   Resumé Makeover

Correct the resumé on page 85 using the format and style that you think would best highlight Jan's experiences. Make up details as needed to make it a winning resumé. Compare it with the annotated resumé on page 86. Finally, look at the makeover resumé on page 87 to see the end result. More examples of winning resumés can be found in the chapter appendix.

Resumé

Jan Winkler
112 Post Street
Ohio Tech College
Lansing, Ohio 49983
724–1058

Sex: Female
Age: 21
Marital Status: Single
Height: 5' 6"
Weight: 142

Job Objective

I want to be an engineer.

Education

Ohio Tech. College, BS in Engineering, 1995

Experience

Rockwell Corp. I worked as a receptionist and telephone operator. I answered the phone, typed letters, wrote proposals, and did data processing.
1994–1995

Sunnybrae Animal Clinic I worked as an assistant to a veterinary and helped out wherever I could.

Awards and Honors

Dean's List
Awarded a scholarship

Community and Campus Activities

Presbyterian Food Bank, volunteer
Big Sisters, Volunteer

References

Dr. John Hines
Sara McRight
Mr. Joshua Livingston

Annotated

Center and bold — Resumé —— Leave off; not necessary

Jan Winkler
112 Post Street
Ohio Tech College
Lansing, Ohio 49983

Need area code — 724-1058

Do not include personal data

Sex: Female
Age: 21
Marital Status: Single
Height: 5' 6"
Weight: 142

Job Objective —— Lack of Caps/bold for headings

Write a specific objective or omit. —— I want to be an engineer.

Spell out degree
Education

Spell out

Ohio Tech. College, BS in Engineering, 1995   Where?   GPA?

Experience

Position? —— Rockwell Corp. I worked as a receptionist and telephone operator. I answered the phone, typed letters, wrote proposals, and did data processing.
1994–1995

Don't use "I"; use action phrases not sentences

Highlight position —— Sunnybrae Animal Clinic I worked as an assistant to a veterinary and helped out wherever I could. Dates?

Awards and Honors —— Put under Education

Dean's List

Not necessary —— Awarded a scholarship —— Name of scholarship

Community and Campus Activities

Presbyterian Food Bank, volunteer —— Inconsistent capitalization
Big Sisters, Volunteer   Campus activities?

References —— Put references on separate page

Use titles for everyone —— Dr. John Hines
Sara McRight
Mr. Joshua Livingston

Jan A. Winkler

College address:
112 Post Street
Lansing, Ohio 49983
(405) 724–1058

Permanent address:
256 Shelter Grove
Lakeside, Ohio 49939
(513) 724–1058

JOB OBJECTIVE:

An entry-level electrical engineering position with a large environmental firm.

EDUCATION:

June 1995 **Bachelor of Science Electrical Engineering**
Ohio Technical College, Lansing, Ohio
Overall GPA: 3.89
Senior Project: Creating Software for customer service

AWARDS AND HONORS:

1994 Business Women's Scholarship
1992–1993 Dean's List at Ohio Technical College

EXPERIENCE:

1994–1995 **Internship**
Rockwell Corporation, Lansing, Ohio
• Created software package for customer
• Answered the phone, typed letters
• Completed data processing entries

1993–1994 **Veterinary Assistant**
Sunnybrae Animal Clinic, Lansing, Ohio
• Assisted with animals
• Cleaned cages and fed animals
• Sterilized surgical instruments

CAMPUS AND COMMUNITY SERVICE

1994–1995 Vice Chair of Engineering Club,
Ohio Technical College
Summer l993 Presbyterian Food Bank (served 50 meals, distributed
260 food baskets)
1992–1993 Big Sisters of Lansing

References
for Jan Winkler

Dr. John Hines
Dean of Advising
Ohio Technical College
112 Post Street
Lansing, Ohio 49983
(405) 726–4021

Ms. Sara McRight
Director of Marketing
Rockwell Corporation
2310 Hopkins Drive
Lansing, Ohio 49983
(405) 722–3104

Mr. Joshua Livingston
Veterinary Assistant
Sunnybrae Animal Clinic
103 12th Street
Lakeside, Ohio 49939
(513) 724–1130

THE BENEFIT FACTOR

Your resumé will be most effective when it is results-oriented and connects your experiences with filling a need in the company. Using action words to translate your experiences into accomplishments will help show how you have benefited the companies where you have worked. Showing the benefit connection with specific accomplishments and results will produce a stronger resumé.

The Benefit Factor

For example:
Administrative Assistant

- Implemented new procedures for business transactions that reduced overhead ($45,000-a-year savings), installed promotional displays, developed weekly reports, and created a new customer satisfaction form.
- Organized Holiday Fundraising Event (earned $120,000).

Based on the example above,

1. How could you translate your skills?
2. What other measures, besides money earned or saved, could be used to assess your skills?

_____

_____

HITTING THE WALL

You have spent hours compiling just the right resumé to highlight your skills and abilities. You may get confused and discouraged at times as you listen to different advice. Some resumé books tell you one thing, career counselors tell you something else, and friends insist that yet another way is best. There is no one right way to write a resumé. Review the chapter strategies and professional advice, use common sense, and then trust yourself to know which style markets your unique personal traits, experience, education, and skills.

Scaling the Wall

You may also get discouraged if you don't get a response from every company to which you sent a resumé. You may, in fact, have to send dozens of resumés to get even a few responses. Don't get discouraged. Think of your resumé as an appealing, concise, fact sheet that lists your main qualifications. Rely more upon building your professional network and making direct personal contacts as effective ways to secure an interview.

Scaling the Wall

Here are a few tips to keep your attitude positive and your motivation high:

- Concentrate on your experience, education, and skills. Don't play the comparison game. FOCUS ON YOUR STRENGTHS.
- Keep a success list: new people you have met, responses you have received, exciting companies you have researched, and your growing network list.
- Set specific goals and priorities every day.
- Stay active and involved. Send out a certain number of resumés each week. Talk with people and follow up on leads.

Imagery: See yourself creating and mailing a well-thought-out resumé that you can be proud of. Imagine yourself setting up job interviews as a result of your hard work.

Positive Self-Talk:

- I have demonstrated solid skills and achievements.
- I find it satisfying and challenging to translate my experiences into an effective resumé.

The Knockout Factor

Your resumé will fail if it

- Is too long and complicated.
- Is messy or has misspelled words.
- Does not emphasize achievements and problem-solving skills.
- Is too flowery and not based on facts.
- Is sent at random, without a cover letter. (See Chapter 4).

The Success Factor

Your resumé will be a winner if it

- Is short, concise, and neat
- Focuses on skills, achievements, and the ability to solve problems and clearly shows a relationship to the available job.
- Is honest, simple, and free of errors.
- Is printed on quality paper and sent with a cover letter.

PROBLEM SOLVING AT WORK

Problem Solving

Amy has just graduated from a career college with a career diploma. She is eager to begin her career as a legal secretary. She is a returning student and has spent most of her adult life raising children and doing volunteer work. She has had little paid work experience. Amy has always considered a resumé something you write when you have had a "real" job. She is worried about how to explain the years she spent in volunteer organizations.

Should she use a functional or chronological resumé? Here is how Amy used creative problem solving to explore solutions and critical thinking in order to make her decision.

1. Have I clearly stated the problems? Should I use traditional, nontraditional, or a combination of job searching methods?

> **Define problem:** I want to write a really good resumé that best reflects my skills and achievements.
>
> **What:** What is my job objective? What resumé format would be most effective? What achievements and skills should I highlight?
>
> **Who:** Whom should I send it to? Whom should I include as references?
>
> **When:** When should I send it?
>
> **Where:** Where do I want to work? To which companies should I send this ?

2. Do I have enough information? Do I have all the information I need to make a decision? Have I researched the benefits of each type of resumé? Have I taken the time to reflect upon my skills and abilities, completed my database, and outlined how my achievements would benefit the company?

3. Can I make the decision by myself? What resources are available to help me make a better decision? Have I talked with a career counselor, my advisor, or my instructors?

4. Have I brainstormed creative alternatives? What other methods are available? Could I highlight my skills and stand out by using a combination resumé?

5. Have I looked at likely consequences? If I create a direct, clear, and professional resumé, will I increase my chances of getting a job? What other consequences might occur if I take the time to reflect upon my achievements and connect my skills with a specific job?

6. Have I identified all the resources and tools needed? Have I researched the resources available? Am I aware of library resources, career centers, computer programs, and instructors that would help me develop better writing skills, develop a professional-looking resumé, and help with proofreading? Am I willing to acquire the additional skills and tools to be successful?

7. Have I developed and implemented an action plan? Have I designed an action plan that will help me make sound decisions?

8. Have I identified the best solution and done everything possible to ensure success? Have I made a decision using critical thinking and creativity? Am I committed to making the decision a success?

9. Have I assessed the results? Have I evaluated my decision to see if it is working? Have I assessed my grades, work satisfaction, and goals? How effective is my resumé and method of distribution? What could I do that would make my job search more effective at this stage?

10. Have I modified the plan, if necessary? What adjustments could I make that would make my decision more successful?

Resumé-Writing Strategies

- Put time and effort into writing an effective resumé.
- Organize the essential information into sections.
- Review your autobiography and data sheets for skills, achievements, and strengths.
- Choose the best format for you.
- Follow the guidelines in this chapter for an effectice resume
- Keep it simple, accurate, and flawless.
- Highlight accomplishments and how you can benefit the company.
- Use action words.

Resumé-Writing Checklist   Yes   No

Have you produced a resumé that has a professional appearance?
Is it

    Neat and clean?
    Error free?
    Grammatically sound?
    On quality paper?
    Professional looking?
    Visually appealing?

Does it have

    Plenty of white space?
    Bold headings?

Have you paid attention to organization?
Does it include

    Address and phone number?
    Chronological format (most recent experience first)?
    Functional format (list skills)?
    Dates?
    Clear, concise, and complete data?
    Centered format?

Is the content of your resumé effective?
Does it contain

    Action-oriented words?
    Action-oriented job statements?
    Emphasis on results and accomplishments?
    Measurable benefits (when possible)?
    Only essential information?
    Honest and factual material?

Appendix: More Good Resumés

The next few pages contain more examples of resumés that are clear, concise, and complete. These models show resumés written in chronological style, functional style, and a combination style. One of these styles will work for you, whether you have a great deal of work experience, little work experience, or have recently re-entered the job market.

Laura L. Lewis
613 Park Avenue
Wales, New York 20992
(914) 621–9882

Education

1991   Maryland Institute of Art   Baltimore, MD
Bachelor of Arts in Commercial/Graphic Arts

Work Experience

1992–present   **Freelance Artist**   Wales, NY
Designed numerous brochures, illustrated posters,
photographed series on food preparation for weekly
magazine. Edited home show articles.

1991–92   Ellis Graphics, Inc.   Baltimore, MD
Graphic Artist and Assistant Editor
Produced printed illustrations, brochures, business cards.
Supervised layout productions, covered home shows.
Planned displays for metropolitan garden show. Responsible
for all layouts, photo displays, and original drawings.
Worked directly with the editor in chief.

1990–91   *National Home and Garden Magazine*   Baltimore, MD
Intern Staff Photographer
Designed setups and photographed homes and gardens.
Illustrated articles on interior design. Photographed indoor
and outdoor scenes and nature close-ups. Edited articles
on interior design. Taught basic photography to staff.

Awards

1992   *Home and Garden Magazine* Creative Photography Award

CRAIG L. CHAMBERLAIN
19 Central Avenue
Cleveland, Ohio 44112

CAREER OBJECTIVE: To acquire a paralegal position that will utilize my administrative, legal, and
computer skills.

WORK EXPERIENCE:

1994–present	Municipal Court of Ohio	Cleveland, OH

Legal Secretary
- Responsible for contract negotiations, preparation of legal documentation and correspondence, mergers, and acquisitions.
- Prepare budget and compile tax filing information. Maintain court calendar.

1993–1994	Allen Stokes and Partners	Cleveland, OH

Paralegal Intern
- Handled pretrial arrangements, drafted summons and complaints, took depositions, drafted court decisions, and researched cases.
- Developed data communication network that increased billing efficiency by 15 percent.

SKILLS

- Fluent in Spanish.
- Proficient in IBM and Apple MAC II.
- Motivated, hardworking self-starter.
- Excellent organizational skills.
- Demonstrated ability to work with diverse clients and co-workers.

EDUCATION

1994	Ohio Career School	Cleveland, OH

Paralegal Studies Degree
Notary Public Training for State of Ohio

Dennis L. Yates
237 Park Lane
Raleigh, North Carolina
(205) 561–1231

EDUCATION

1995	DUKE UNIVERSITY	Raleigh, NC

Bachelor of Science in Occupational Therapy
- Grade Point Average 3.8/4.0
- Academic Dean's List
- Earned 100 percent of college costs

WORK EXPERIENCE

1994–95	DUKE UNIVERSITY HOSPITAL	Raleigh, NC

Intern Occupational Therapist
- Specialized in pediatrics play therapy. Worked with developmentally delayed, autistic, learning disabled, and cerebral palsy patients. Developed schedules, assisted with treatment, motivated and coached patients.

1992–93	MENTAL HEALTH CENTER	Raleigh, NC

Medical Secretary
- Performed research, filed reports, typed, entered data processing.
- Installed and trained staff in database computer system. Resulted in reduction of estimated 12 hours per week of reporting.

MEMBERSHIPS AND COMMUNITY SERVICE

- American Occupational Therapy Association
- Sunset Senior Citizens Home: Assisted Director in developing and implementing programs.

EMILY CHAN
902 12th Street
Grand Lakes, Minnesota 55002

CAREER SUMMARY: Accounting supervisor with eight years experience in accounting, computer systems, and administration.

EMPLOYMENT HISTORY

1992–present Rockford Company   Grand Lakes, MN
Accounting Supervisor
Responsible for all accounting functions.
Accomplishments:
- Designed and implemented computer-based accounting system. Saved 20 percent of accountants' workload.
- Developed new training program for audit programs and wrote procedure booklet.
- Secured $150,000 grant for worker training.

1990–1992 Trenton Accounting Agency   Trenton, MN
Accountant
Analyzed all accounting records and budgets.

Accomplishments:
- Designed computer payroll system.
- Redesigned reporting procedures to comply with new state and federal regulations.

EDUCATION

1990 TRENTON STATE COLLEGE, Trenton, MN
Bachelor of Science in Accounting

1991 Certified Public Accountant, Minnesota (passed first time)

1991 Trenton Community College, Trenton, MN
Continuing Education Computer Science Program

AFFILIATIONS AND MEMBERSHIPS

1990–present American Association of Accountants
1992–present Trenton Business and Professional Women
1993 President, Trenton State College Accounting Club
1994 American Cancer Society Board of Directors

Jan A. Berg
354 Pinehill Street
Aspen, Colorado 83992
(607) 839–2883

EDUCATION

1995   MOUNTAINVIEW COLLEGE   Aspen, CO
Bachelor of Science in Industrial Technology
Management emphasis with focus on manufacturing
processes, quality control, CAD/CAM, industrial design,
and materials science.

Business minor—Course work emphasis on statistics,
finance, economics, accounting, management.

SKILLS

- Skilled in interpersonal communication.
- Proficient in Macintosh and DOS formats and a variety of
  software, including spreadsheets, word processing,
  database.
- Hardworking, self-motivated, and positive.
- Demonstrated ability to work effectively in teams.

EMPLOYMENT HISTORY

1994–present INSTITUTE FOR INDUSTRIAL TECHNOLOGY   Aspen, CO
Personal Assistant to Vice President
- Prepare cost estimates, contracts, and regular progress
  reports. Set weekly agenda.
- Review and modify work performance forms.
- Created employee database system improving efficiency
  and reliability in scheduling. Increased profits by 15
  percent in one year.

1993–1994   INSTITUTE FOR INDUSTRIAL TECHNOLOGY
Intern Manufacturing Staff
- Interacted with clients, researched needs, and developed
  industrial designs.
- Assisted in advertisement and promotional program.

AFFILIATIONS

1993–present Industrial Technology Institute

Thomas R. Kason
903 Grenwood Lane
Bennet, Maine 01223

MECHANICAL SKILLS:

Brake systems	Electrical systems
Front ends	Tire rotation
Engine tune-up	Electrical fuel injection
Heating	Air conditioning
Engine performance	Shock absorbers

CUSTOMER RELATIONS AND SALES:

- Excellent rapport with customers.
- Designed successful customer satisfaction form to improve service and feedback.
- Motivated and hardworking (increased sales by 25 percent in one year).
- Improved repeat customers (over 15 percent increase).

WORK EXPERIENCE:

1992–present MELVIN'S AUTO SHOP
Mechanic
- Diagnose and repair various vehicles.
- Responsible for body work, tune-ups, ignition repair, transmission repair, and maintenance.
- Develop a good working relationship with customers. Prepare billings and follow up on customer concerns.

EDUCATION:

1994 BENNET COMMUNITY COLLEGE   Bennet, ME
Associate of Science Degree
Automotive Technology
GPA 3.6/4.0

CERTIFICATE:

1995 STERLING TRAINING PROGRAMS
Certificate of Training on Foreign Cars

Maria M. Perez
2839 Elm Drive
Evans, Illinois 80392
(702) 883–1231

TECHNICAL SKILLS

Knowledge of:
- Key Systems
- Network Topologies
- Software Lotus, MS/DOS

Experience with:
- Traffic Analysis
- Digital Multimeters
- Query System Setup

CUSTOMER SERVICE SKILLS

- Effective team skills (Managed two college team projects)
- Ability to work with variety of people
- Effective written and oral communication (Published senior project)
- Creative problem solving (Solved traffic analysis problem)
- Hardworking and persistent: Worked 40 hours a week while attending school at night

WORK EXPERIENCE

1993–1994 **Data Entry Clerk,** Baylor Corp., Evans, IL
1993 **Intern Telecommunications Specialist,** Baylor Corp., Evans, IL

EDUCATION

June 1993 Redwoods Institute of Technology, Evans, IL
Associate of Science
Major: Telecommunications
Minor: Computer Science
GPA 3.6

SENIOR PROJECT

Systems Documentation and Network for a Telecommunications Company

CHAPTER 4

Writing Your Cover Letter and Application

I have made this letter longer than usual, only because I have not had the time to make it shorter.

Blaise Pascal 1657

Activity level is the most important determinant of job hunting success. Finders out-hustle non-finders by double or triple the level of activity.

Kenneth Cole, publisher
The Recruiting Search Report

Introduction

Many serious job hunters put a great deal of time into writing a great resumé and preparing for the interview but write a quick and general cover letter as an afterthought—if they send one at all. Companies are often bombarded with hundreds of unsolicited resumés (IBM receives over a million resumés a year), yet few are accompanied by well-written, specific cover letters. For many people, writing a cover letter is intimidating. But writing a simple, specific, targeted, and personalized letter is a great job-search strategy that produces results.

—

Learning Objectives

In Chapter 4, you will learn

- The importance of the cover letter.

- How to write an effective letter.

- How to complete an application form.

- How to prepare for employment tests.

The Importance of the Cover Letter

An effective cover letter greatly increases your chances of being asked for an interview. Your resumé should be general enough so that you can use it to apply for a number of jobs, but your cover letter should be specific to each job. The purpose of the cover letter is to entice your reader to take a close look at your resumé. It should also communicate your purpose, enthusiasm, intelligence, energy, drive, and your unique abilities and personal qualities. Always send a cover letter whenever you send a resumé.

A cover letter is written to introduce your resumé, focus your skills, identify your job objective, indicate your enthusiasm, illustrate that you've done your homework, and add a personal touch. In addition, as with any business letter, it serves as a record. Always keep a copy for your files.

An effective cover letter can be one of the most important factors in getting a job interview. If the cover letter is dull or sloppy, it can ruin your chances for an interview. Since communication skills are among the most important skills you can bring to a job, a cover letter is your opportunity to demonstrate that you can write in a clear, concise, and direct manner.

An effective cover letter

1. Creates a positive first impression. Begin by telling the employer why you are applying for the position. You want to make an immediate good impression. Your personality and a sense of warmth should shine through.

2. States your accomplishments. You want to list one or two main accomplishments. Tell what you have done that has made a difference.

3. States the benefit factor. State how your skills can meet the company's needs. This indicates that you have done your research on both the organization and the specific office that you are interested in and that you know what the employer is looking for in an employee. You want to show how you can contribute to the company's success.

4. Indicates that you are a problem solver. Describe how you have used creativity or critical thinking to solve problems and make sound decisions. Employers value employees who are creative problem solvers.

5. Shows initiative and confidence. The letter should state when you will call to set up an interview. This shows that you are a take charge person who will follow up on details.

The Difference between a Successful Cover Letter and the One That Gets Tossed Aside

A successful cover letter

- Has all the necessary structural elements: date, inside address, salutation, body, closing, and signature.
- Contains no more than two to four paragraphs.
- Has short, action-oriented, concise paragraphs.
- Includes complete name and title of person who will receive the letter.
- Personally communicates to the employer why you are attracted to the company and indicates your personal qualities and warmth.
- Demonstrates that you've done your homework.
- Indicates how you can benefit the company.
- Relates your skills so that they match the company's needs point by point.
- Reflects your enthusiasm and indicates that you are willing to put in the effort to be successful.
- Points out specific aspects of your resumé.

Guidelines for Better Letters

Job-search letters should not be written as an isolated event. Effective letters are only one component of a group of interrelated tasks that work together in the job-search process. It is difficult to write an effective letter if you have not researched the companies you would like to work for. Your research should also identify the person who is doing the hiring for the position you are interested in. Networking with friends, professionals you have met at trade associations, friends of friends, and contacts in the business community will help you find out more about the company and the names and titles of key people. By now you are aware of how interconnected the job search steps are. Time spent assessing your skills, interests, values, and achievements; researching occupations, jobs, and companies; identifying your career goals and objectives; networking; and writing a professional resumé will pay big dividends at this stage of the job search. Your letters should flow from and be linked to all of these steps as you navigate the career path. If you are having difficulty writing a cover letter, you may want to go back to earlier steps and clarify your values, interests, accomplishments, and goals, and how you would benefit potential employers.

Your cover letter creates an image that reflects who you are. The following guidelines can help you create a professional image. Your cover letter is a business letter and should be:

Researched

All good writing starts by deciding on your purpose and analyzing the audience. Research the company and decide what needs exist. You can then show how your background can meet these needs. Tailor each letter to a specific job.

Complete

As illustrated in the sample letter on the next page, a business letter essentially contains seven parts:

1. Letterhead or return address.
2. Date.
3. Inside address.
4. Salutation.
5. Body.
6. Complimentary close.
7. Signature.

Interesting

The letter should get the reader's attention, create interest, and be action-oriented. Keep the reader's interest by varying sentence length and structure. Keep your tone warm, yet professional. This is a formal business letter.

Brief

Keep letters to one page. Concentrate on the jobs that best demonstrate your accomplishments and skills. Brevity is important. It shows that you respect how busy the reader is and that you are capable of writing in a clear, simple, and concise manner.

Addressed to a specific person

Always address your letter to a specific person whenever possible. Generally, a phone call to the targeted company will give you the name, title, and correct spelling of the person hiring.

Focused on your benefit to the company

Your letter should be employer-centered, not self-centered. Highlight your accomplishments and skills and relate them to how you will benefit the company through this specific job.

Positive and confident

Your tone, choice of words, and content should suggest a positive, productive, and optimistic person. Don't convey doubt or uncertainty with words such as, *sort of, hope, guess, think, wish.*

Action-oriented

Action words, such as the ones used in your resumé (see page 71), create a powerful letter. Indicate that you will call.

Honest

Make certain you can back up, give specific examples of, and demonstrate all your accomplishments.

Error free

Proofread each letter for spelling and other errors. Your letter should be flawless.

Professional looking

Always invest in quality bond paper with matching envelopes. Use off-white, beige, or grey. A word processor or computer will give your letter a professional look and make it easier to change your letter to specifically fit each job.

The following are examples of excellent cover letters. The numbers shown to the left of each letter are for explanatory purposes only.

1.

John L. McAllen
2910 Greenbriar Lane, Troy, Michigan 48002

2. April 3, 199_

3. Mr. Brian Shaw
Director of Marketing
National Creative Sales, Incorporated
322 Blossom Street
Jackson, Texas 43318

4. Dear Mr. Shaw:

5. It was with enthusiasm that I read your ad requesting applications for a sales representative. My background matches all of your ad's requirements. My job objective is to use my persuasive skills and organizational and marketing abilities in sales.

Your requirements are for a person who can increase sales accounts. My skills and experience are ideally suited and applicable to the requirements for sales representative and include these accomplishments:

- Created a customer service program.
- Won the Outstanding Sales Award.
- Increased sales by 40 percent through effective communication, service, and hard work.
- Increased my accounts from 50 to 70 accounts without adding cost.
- Won 1992 Innovation Award for creation and implementation of sales campaign.

I also have experience in publicity, public relations, and customer service. While going to school, I held down a part-time job and volunteered in the community. I am hard working and dependable. If we could meet, I am certain that you would agree that my winning spirit and commitment to customers could greatly benefit your company. I will call next week to arrange an interview at your convenience.

6. Sincerely,

7. John L. McAllen

1. 190 Rose Lane
Kalamazoo, Michigan 49007

2. March 26,1996

3. Mr. Arthur Shaw, Director of Sales
National Creative Sales Company
992 Timmons Street
Petersburg, North Dakota

4. Dear Mr. Shaw:

5. I have read the annual report for the National Creative Sales Company. The growth rate of 23% is impressive, indeed! You have developed and marketed fine products and I am delighted to know that your new sport line is also doing well. I am interested in contributing my marketing, organizational, and persuasive skills to a progressive company in a sales position which offers substantial challenge. National Creative Sales is a growing company with an excellent reputation. I would like to contribute to its success.

Throughout college and during the summers, I have worked in the area of sales and have progressively increased my sales and marketing skills. In June, I will graduate with an Associate's Degree in Marketing and want to continue in the area of sales. I have:

- Demonstrated excellent communication, organizational, and team skills.
- Handled customer complaints and solved concerns of major customers.
- Developed a program to spot and solve company's customer service complaints.

As an intern project, I have developed some marketing materials that I think would fit in perfectly with your latest campaign. I have earned the reputation of being a team player and spreading goodwill where ever I have worked. I will call you next Tuesday to see if a meeting could be arranged to discuss these exciting ideas. In the meantime, if you would like to contact me, my number is (408) 521-2370.

6. Sincerely,

7. Mary Gearly

The following guidelines cover each part of a successful cover letter and give you an opportunity to practice. The section numbers correspond to the numbers shown on the preceding cover letters.

Seven Steps to a Successful Cover Letter

Like a resumé, a cover letter can be broken down into sections, each one with its own purpose. There are seven sections in a successful cover letter:

Section 1. Letterhead or Return Address

When you are preparing a cover letter on plain paper (using the block format), type the return address approximately two inches from the top of the page, single-spaced, and flush left. Don't use abbreviations.

You can have your stationery printed with your letterhead at the top or type it yourself. Make certain it is centered. This will make your cover letter look professional. You can also type your address immediately below your name as part of the signature block.

2910 Greenbriar Lane
Troy, Michigan 48002

Section 2. Date

The date is typed directly below the return address. If you use letterhead paper, type the date three to five spaces below the last line of the printed or typed letterhead. If you used plain paper and you type the return address as part of the signature block, type the date six spaces (two inches) from the top of the page.

2910 Greenbriar Lane
Troy, Michigan 48002

April 19, 1995

Section 3. Inside Address

An inside address is essential for business correspondence. Type it on the left, four to six spaces below the date. Make certain you have the correct title, address, and spelling. For example:

Dr. Albert L. Ferroro
Dean of Graduate Studies
Alberta Career School
1324 Elmwood Avenue
Alberta, Michigan 48821

Section 4. Salutation

The salutation begins with *Dear,* includes such titles as Mr., Mrs., Ms., Miss, and Dr., and ends with a colon(:). (For the appropriate forms of address for government or church officials, see the appendix of Webster's New World Dictionary.) You should call first and find out whom you should address the cover letter to and what his or her title is. Occasionally, you may not know a person's name. In this case, only capitalize the *Dear* since the title is general. For example, Dear public relations director:

Dear Dr. Ferroro:

EXERCISE 4.1   **Starting Your Cover Letter**

Write out your letterhead, date, return address, and salutation.

_____

_____

_____

_____

_____

Section 5. Body

The First Paragraph: Capture Attention

Single-space the body of the letter with double spaces between paragraphs. Use the block format so that every paragraph starts at the left margin, as shown in the sample letter.

The first paragraph should introduce you and your purpose for writing. This is the place to clearly state your job objective. Capture the employer's attention by describing why you are interested in the job. Demonstrate that you have done your homework and know a few things about the company.

The Second Paragraph: Create Interest

The second paragraph should get the reader interested in meeting you. It should briefly highlight your skills and accomplishments and relate them point by point to the job you're applying for. Use action words to highlight your skills and abilities without appearing self-centered. Use the word *you* whenever possible. For example:

Your annual report indicates you are expanding in the area of sales. You may find that my expertise in sales and customer relations is just what you need.

Don't state a salary requirement even if the ad requests it. You can simply say that the salary should be comparable to other professionals in your field with your experience and education. Remember, you do not want anything to keep you from the all-important interview. Too high a salary requirement and they may reject you; too low and they may wonder about your worth.

The Final Paragraph: Action

In the final paragraph, indicate what the next step will be. Never be vague or put the action in the employer's court. Close by saying that you will call in a few days. Don't request an interview or ask them to call you. You want to show initiative and drive. Tell the person that you will be calling on a certain date to discuss an interview. Make certain you follow up.

Section 6. Complimentary Close

The complimentary close is the formal end of the letter and is typed two spaces below the last line of your final paragraph. It should be capitalized and followed by a comma. Complimentary closings used in business include *Sincerely, Cordially, Yours Truly,* and *Respectfully.*

Section 7. Signature

Leave four or five spaces for your signature after the closing . Type your full name. Professional titles or degrees may be typed after your name but are not included in your signature. Write your signature in a legible, careful manner, using a good pen. Take care not to scrawl your name.

Sincerely,

John L. McAllen

John L. McAllen

EXERCISE 4.2   **Outlining the Body**

Jot down the outline of a "typical" cover letter—what common item will you always want to highlight in generic cover letters? Use page 129 at the end of the chapter to write a complete draft of a generic cover letter showing all seven parts.

_____

_____

_____

_____

_____

_____

Helpful Hints

Margins and Spacing.

Margins vary depending on the length of the letter. Letters should be centered with at least a one-inch margin on all sides. Most word-processing programs have a preset margin that can be used for most letters. If typing a short letter (under 100 words), insert extra line spaces at the top of the page and between the date and inside address so that your letter looks centered. When using the block format, single-space your text and double-space between paragraphs and when introducing a list. If you want to use a modified block format, indent each new line of a paragraph five spaces.

Word Processing

Use a word processor so that you can easily make corrections and update your cover letter, often. Your letter should not have any errors or correction fluid. Your cover letter reflects you and you want it to look neat, clean, and professional.

Accuracy is Important

Make sure your cover letter is accurate! When in doubt about grammar, usage, and spelling, double-check a dictionary or grammar handbook. Here are a few useful rules:

Capitalization

Capitalize proper nouns (people, places, and things):

- Senator Jones.
- Yreka, California.
- Red Cross.
- The Southwest (specific geographical location).
- How to Start Your Own Business (Capitalize and underline titles of books and magazines).
- Jello (Capitalize trademarks).
- Dr. Jones, Vice President of Academic Affairs (Specific title).

Don't capitalize:

- Titles unless they are specific. For example, Dr. Jones is a competent vice president of academic affairs.
- Seasons (spring, fall).
- Points on the compass. (Drive south and then north.)

Abbreviations

Limit the use of abbreviations in your cover letter and resumé.

- College degrees: instead of B.A. use (Bachelor of Art), B.S. use (Bachelor of Science), M.A. (Master of Arts), M.B.A. (Master of Business Administration); Ph.D., J.D., C.P.A., etc., should always be abbreviated.
- Most abbreviated words are followed by a period (Jr.).
- When states are abbreviated do *not* use a period (WA).
- The abbreviation of et cetera, (etc.) is always preceded and followed by a comma, unless it ends a sentence. I have experience using office equipment, such as copy machines, fax machines, computers, etc.

Apostrophe

Use an apostrophe to indicate one or more omitted letters:

In general, it is best to limit the use of apostrophes since the cover letter is a formal business letter.

- It's (It is) time to follow up on phone calls.
- Don't (Do not) wear inappropriate clothes to a job interview.
- They're (They are) interested in good manners.

Use an apostrophe to indicate possession:

- The company's profits rose by 23 percent.
- I had the honor of being a President's scholar.

Usage

They're, their, and there

- They're (They are) going to set up an interview for Friday.
- Their offices are in Sieman's Hall.
- There are many job opportunities available.

Lay and lie

- Lay the book down.
- Lie down and rest.

Principal and principle

- The principal gave me a letter of reference. The principal is a pal.
- His principles are of the highest integrity.

Avoid Common Mistakes

- **Misspelled words.** Make certain that your letter has correct spelling. Errors are unforgivable and reveal you as incompetent and sloppy. Besides using a spell checker, ask someone else to check your letter over.
- **Too long.** Your letter should be concise, crisp, and to the point. Don't waste the employer's time.
- **Too general.** Your letter should be written for a certain position, addressed to a specific individual, and should summarize outstanding skills and accomplishments. Don't address a letter *To whom it may concern.* Make certain you have the person's correct title, name, and address.
- **Lists too many duties.** Don't summarize your resumé, use dates, or try to cover all of your previous duties. Explain one or two of your most outstanding accomplishments.
- **Focuses on your needs.** You should focus on the needs of the company, not on your needs or wishes. What can you do to benefit the company?
- **Uses gimmicks.** Don't try to be cute or resort to gimmicks. Respect the intelligence and dignity of your reader.
- **Is weak, insecure, and boring.** Don't be unduly modest. You want to show confidence and self-assurance and allow your personality to come across. Don't sound as if you are desperate or so needy for a job that you will take anything. Use a strong ending. Don't wait for the employer to call you. Set a time to call.
- **Has a passive tone.** Choose your words carefully to show action and energy. Some of these are listed on page 71.
- **Is disjointed and aimless.** Your words and style should indicate that you are organized, have a purpose, and can write logically. State the purpose of the letter and your career goal.
- **Is messy and unprofessional looking.** Make certain your letter is flawless and produced on quality paper. Your envelope should match. You want to make a good impression. Go first-class.

No Specific Job in Mind?

(The "Blind" Cover Letter)

In many cases, you may not be applying for a specific job, but you want to write to companies you would like to work for or you want to follow up on contacts you have met through networking. This cover letter is a response to a networking contact and goes with the resumé on page 99.

903 Greenwood Lane
Bennet, Maine 01223

October 29, 199_

Mr. John Tempis
231 Brook Street, John's Texaco Station
Bennet, Maine 01223

Dear Mr. Tempis:

It was a pleasure to talk with you yesterday. I appreciate your taking the time to discuss the field of auto mechanics and have enclosed a resumé for your review and evaluation. As we discussed, auto mechanics is my chosen occupation and my passion. I have worked on cars since I was 11 years old and have developed a reputation for customer satisfaction. I recently earned a certificate in foreign car engine repair.

Your station has grown in the last two years and has a reputation for being customer-service oriented. In addition to excellent technical skills, I have demonstrated a willingness to help customers and build good relationships. My accomplishments include:

• Designing a customer satisfaction form.
• Increasing sales by 25 percent.
• Never being late for work in two years.
• Earning a reputation for being dependable and hardworking.

I have hands-on experience with solving problems in the automobile business and in increasing sales. If you know of openings at your company or other opportunities that may exist for a self-starter, please let me know. Thanks again for taking time to meet with me.

Sincerely,

Thomas R. Kason

EXERCISE 4.3   Respond to Ad

Using one of the following job advertisements as the basis for a job you're applying to, create an accurate and complete focused cover letter in the space on page 130. Don't forget the seven parts.

HELP WANTED

Chiropractic Assistant

Full-time position available. Must be good with people and paperwork, and have a positive mental attitude and good communication skills. Will provide training. Send resumé and references to

Dr. John Fullerton, Box 349 Riverton, Ohio 43998.

HELP WANTED

Accounting Technician

Fortuna Union High School District is accepting applications for a full-time Accounting Technician. Payroll, accounts payable, and benefits experience required. Salary: $2,028/mo. Applications and job descriptions available from business office at

14th St. Fortuna, Maine 01276.

EXERCISE 4.4   Cover Letter Makeover

Review all the mistakes made in this cover letter and correct them.

May 19, 199_

Global Service Industry
South Street
Boston, MA

Dear Sir,

Don't read another resumé! You have found yourself the perfect employee for a job as automotive technician or in sales.

It has been my pleasure to have had many years of experience working in the automotive field as a technician, mechanic, and salesman. I have a real interest in living in the Boston area. I love the ocean and cultural events, too. I have a strong background in elect., mechanics, and PR.

I would like a position of authority where I can learn more about sales and public relations. I have worked for Bob Knells of Shell station for 3 years (from 1991 to 1994). Bob and I were friends and he allowed me to deal with customers, put out fires, work on various cars and trucks, and I had input on advertisement. Unfortately Bob was hard to work for so I quit. Now I work for my uncle.

I am sorry that this letter does not reflect my best effort. My typewriter is worn and I didn't have time to have it typed professionally or even to buy better paper.

Here is my address and you can call me at work anytime—738-9937.

Hoping for a interview
Jud Meyers

EXERCISE 4.5 Compare

Compare this direct contact letter to the previous letter written by Jud.
Any more suggestions?

3452 Tilton Avenue
Niles, New Hampshire 21102

May 19, 199_

Ms. Gloria Webb
Vice President of Sales
Global Service Industry
221 South Street
Boston, MA 08771

Dear Ms. Webb:

I read in the March issue of *Auto Journal* that Global Service has a wonderful
new line of automobiles. The following achievements demonstrate my
commitment to sales:

- Possess technical plus sales experience.
- Exceeded my quoted by 68 percent for last year.
- Named salesperson of the year in 1994.
- Developed a follow-up plan to ensure customer satisfaction.
- Persuaded company to start training program for sales.
- Paid 100 percent of my business school cost.

My background as a skilled automotive technician and mechanic have made
me a better salesman. I love selling and have demonstrated excellent human
relations and communication skills. I want to set new records in sales. I feel
confident that I could really excel and make a contribution to the company.

I have the skills, the passion, and the talent to produce results. I can be
reached at (213)445–2365. I will call you next week to request a meeting at
your convenience.

Sincerely,

Jud E. Meyers

THE BENEFIT FACTOR:
Creative Problem Solving and Decision Making

Since every job involves problem solving and decision making, you will stand out if you can indicate how you have solved problems, increased profits, or reduced spending. Make certain your letter is employer centered and states what you can do for the company.
Use phrases like the ones below:

The Benefit Factor

> With my organizational skills and your product, we can be a winning team.

> Because we know it pays to invest in customer service, I would like to put my human relations skills to work to keep customers satisfied.

> Both of us have the same vision for Computer World. I would love the opportunity to work with you to accomplish our goals.

> Since we both know that personnel matters can be time-consuming and a big source of headaches, my experience can benefit the company.

> 1. How do your skills reflect creativity?
> 2. Can you demonstrate your ability to make decisions?

THE CONTINGENT WORKFORCE

Workplace Trends

Key: Flexibility
A major trend in today's workforce is the growing number of contingent workers. A quarter of today's workforce are employed on a temporary, part-time, free-lance, and contract basis. This trend is known as outsourcing. Most of these employees would rather work full time but find themselves a part of the growing transient workforce. Companies see the advantages of outsourcing—lack of benefits alone can save 40 percent of labor costs. A contingent workforce is more flexible, and flexibility is what today's businesses want. When costs must be cut, hours can be reduced; and when business sags, temporaries are the first to go. This avoids layoffs of permanent employees.

The number of employees working part-time or on a temporary basis has grown by 2.2 million in the last two decades. Some employers think that what contingent workers lack in loyalty, they make up for in quality work. Since they work on a project-by-project basis, contingent workers know they can be replaced if their work isn't outstanding.

Temporary workers have expanded from the traditional secretarial pool to the itinerant executive. There is a growing number of troubleshooting executives hired to clean house and revive ailing companies. This job almost always involves cost cutting and reducing staff.

The new contingent worker will continue to be a major player in the workforce and a reminder that unconditional, full-time, lifelong employment with one company is a thing of the past.
Career Strategies: Develop diverse, marketable skills. Be flexible and take risks.

Job Applications

During the job search, you will probably fill out an application. Once you have a good working sample, it will be easy for you to complete others and to update them. Your database (Chapter 1) includes information that is required on most applications.

An application is similar to a resumé in that, while it won't get you the job, it can keep you from getting an interview. The application is often the employer's first glimpse of you. Therefore, it should create a positive and professional image. The most common mistake is to fill out an application in a hurry, guessing at dates, addresses, or work-history data. But if you carry your database with you, you know that the information you put on an application will be accurate. Make certain you double-check dates. Both the application and your resumé will usually become part of your permanent file if you are hired.

Follow these guidelines for completing a job application:

1. Read carefully. Read through the application and follow directions. Some applications instruct you to print in ink; others will ask you to type. Some applications ask for last name first. Applications vary, so don't assume and start writing before you read the directions. Read every question before you answer.

2. Be accurate. Don't guess. Have your database and resumé on hand to check dates so you can answer questions easily and accurately.

3. Be neat. Buy a couple of fine-point blue or black pens to prevent blots and smears. Fill in blanks carefully. Check to see the amount of space available so you don't run over into the next blank space.

4. Be complete. Answer all questions that are applicable. However, if the question does not apply to you, use a dash (–) or print N/A (not applicable). This will indicate that you have read the question but that it does not apply to you. You can also write in a blank space, "see attached" and then attach appropriate material or write, "Will explain in interview."

5. Be professional. Use your full name. Don't use a nickname.

6. Include job title. Print the name of the job you are applying for or your job objective.

7. Be selective. List only full-time jobs unless you have little work experience or the part-time jobs are related to the job you are applying for. You don't want to list every baby-sitting or lawn-mowing job.

8. List volunteer work. List volunteer, internship, and co-op (educational/work programs in cooperation with business) programs. They indicate a willingness to contribute and get involved.

9. Be flexible. Indicate that you are willing to travel, relocate, or work various shifts.

10. Include references. Make certain you have names, titles, addresses, and phone numbers of references and that you have asked their permission before you include them on the application. Bring your list of references with you.

11. Be positive. Always tell the truth, but don't list disabilities or weaknesses unless specifically asked to. Never be negative about former employers.

12. Check carefully. After completing the application read through it carefully to make certain the information is correct and neat. Check for spelling, grammar, and punctuation. Enter the correct date and sign in your best handwriting.

13. Make a copy. If possible, before filling out the application, make a copy in case you make a mistake. Make a copy of the completed application to use as a guide for other applications.

E X E R C I S E   4 . 6   Application Practice

Practice filling out the sample job application on page 126–28, using the information from your database.

Job Testing

Throughout this book, preparedness has been stressed, both for finding a job and for job success. You will want to continue this thinking and be ready to excel at whatever requirements are necessary.

Certain office or retail positions may include tests in basic math or calculations, typing, shorthand, data entry, word processing, punctuation, spelling, composition, or problem solving. Some jobs also require a physical examination that may include both drug and alcohol testing. You can find this out by calling personnel offices of interested companies, calling job placement agencies, and asking your instructors in the field you are studying.

Before the Test

Be prepared for skill tests that are part of certain jobs. If you are in a secretarial or business course, save your key books and ask your instructor for additional testing materials that may be required before you are interviewed for a position. When you inquire about the job, ask if there are required tests and practice before you take them. Employment agencies often have sample tests that can help you prepare. Knowing what to expect and spending time reviewing will help you to relax, and you will do better on the test.

During the Test

Ask the person in charge for special instructions. For example, if you make a mistake, can you repeat a portion of the test? Can you repeat the entire test and, if so, how many times?

Read through the entire test quickly before you begin answering questions, to get an idea of the content and how much weight is given to each section. Read each question carefully. Ask questions and make certain you know what is being expected.

HITTING THE WALL

Scaling the Wall

Researching each company you are interested in applying to and writing a neat, attractive, and specific cover letter for each resumé that you send takes time and discipline. You also have to face the fear of rejection. Some employers you call for an interview will decline; some will say they will call back, but they won't. It is easy to get discouraged and use lack of time as an excuse for not doing your homework, hastily preparing a cover letter, or not following up with a phone call. It is tempting to sit and wait for an employer to take the initiative and call you. Don't take rejection personally. This is the business world; you have to take the initiative and be confident in your abilities and skills.

It is important to write a direct and personalized cover letter for each company to which you send your resumé. If a company is worth applying to, it is worth writing a cover letter that makes such a positive first impression that the employer will want to meet you in person. Don't hit the wall at this point. Keep up your energy and enthusiasm.

Scaling the Wall

Sometimes even confident people feel inadequate when it comes to writing business letters. Many people face writer's block as they face a blank sheet of paper.

Here are some tips for overcoming writer's block:

- Practice. Write letters often. Look for examples of good letters and keep a file.
- Focus on your job objective and state it clearly. This will give you a sense of purpose, and you will feel more positive and goal directed.
- Get started. Write a quick draft in 10 minutes. Some people react to the stress of writing by procrastinating. Avoid this if at all possible!
- Revise and get feedback from others.

The Knockout Factor

Your cover letter will fail if it:
- Looks unprofessional or is poorly typed.
- Has awkward language and spelling or grammatical errors.
- Neglects to connect your skills, abilities, and accomplishments with the needs of the company.
- Is passive and dull.
- Fails to describe your objective or purpose.
- Fails to indicate that you will call for an interview.
- Is too boastful, aggressive or hyped.

The Success Factor

Your cover letter will succeed if it:
- Looks professional and is neatly typed.
- Is clear, direct, grammatically correct, and free of errors.
- Indicates how your education and accomplishments fit the requirements for the job opening.
- Engages the reader's attention.
- States your specific job objective and purpose.
- States when you will call for an interview.
- Is professional and businesslike.

PROBLEM SOLVING AT WORK

Problem Solving

Jason is a recent graduate with a certificate and Associate of Science Degree in Computer Technology. He has sent out hundreds of resumés but has received only a few interview appointments. Most companies have not even acknowledged receiving his resumé. He hasn't developed a cover letter because he hates writing and thinks that in technical fields, a resumé should provide enough information.

Jason has listed his career objective as a computer programmer at a large corporation. He thought he would be able to get a job more easily at a large company than at a small one. He is now wondering if his objective is too narrow.

Should he write a specific cover letter for each job? Help Jason explore ways to write a cover letter that is specific, interesting, and attention getting for working in a large company. Here's a sample problem-solving script to help Jason make a sound decision.

1. Have I clearly stated the problem? Should I write a specific cover letter for each job?

> **Define problem:** I want to write a really good cover letter that best reflects my skills and achievements and that will help me get a job as a computer programmer. Should I send a specific cover letter for each job?
>
> **What:** What can I say that will clearly state my objective and reflect my skills and abilities? What achievements and skills should I highlight?
>
> **Who:** Who should I send the cover letter to? Should I apply to small as well as large companies?
>
> **When:** When should I send it?
>
> **Where:** Where do I want to work? Which companies should I send this to?

2. Do I have enough information? Do I have all the information I need to make a decision? Have I researched both small and large companies? Have I thought how my skills and accomplishments would relate to and benefit a company? How can I best highlight them in a cover letter? Have I explored the advantages of tailoring a cover letter for each job?

3. Can I make the decision by myself? What resources are available to help me make a better decision? Have I talked with a career counselor, my advisor, or my instructors?

4. Have I brainstormed alternatives? Have I creatively explored alternatives? What are the benefits of working for small and large companies?

5. Have I looked at likely consequences? If I create a concise, direct, and specific cover letter for each job, will I increase my chances of getting a job? What other consequences might occur if I learn to write an effective cover letter that relates my skills and accomplishments to a specific job?

6. Have I identified all the resources and tools needed? Have I researched the resources available? What classes, instructors, career centers, and job-search books that would help me develop better writing skills? Am I willing to acquire the additional skills and tools to be successful?

7. Have I developed and implemented an action plan?

Have I designed an action plan that will help me make sound decisions?

8. Have I identified the best solution and done everything possible to ensure success?

Have I made a decision using critical thinking and creativity? Am I committed to making the decision a success?

9. Have I assessed the results?

Have I evaluated my decision to see if it is working? Have I assessed the results of my plan and how they fit with my goals?

10. Have I modified the plan, if necessary?

What adjustments could I make that would make my decision more successful?

Effective Cover Letter Strategies

- Send a cover letter with every resumé.
- State your job objective.
- Indicate that you have done your homework on the company and mention specifics.
- Relate the needs of employer to your skills and accomplishments.
- Show how your skills can benefit the company.
- Keep your letter concise, neat, action-oriented, and concrete.
- Make certain the job application is neat and correct. Follow directions carefully.

Chapter Checklist   Yes   No

1. **Have you effectively organized your cover letter?**
Is it:
    Tailor-made for each job?
    Addressed to specific name and title of person?
    Comprised of essential information?
    Professionally typed?
    Grammar and error free?
    Concise three or four paragraphs?
    Written in the correct format?
    Printed on quality paper?

2. **Have you paid close attention to content?**
Does it:
    Mention the referral, where you saw the ad, or the purpose of the letter?
    State job objective or area of interest?
    Summarize work and education?
    Use action words?
    Indicate that you've done your homework about the company by citing specifics?
    Match your skills and the job description point by point?
    Tell them you will call?

3. **Have you carefully completed the job application?**
Is it:
    Filled out completely?
    Neat and clean?
    Printed carefully or professionally typed?
    Checked for spelling and grammar?
    Honest, truthful, and accurate?

4. **Are you prepared for job testing?**
Have you:
    Prepared and reviewed?
    Practiced taking various job tests?

SAMPLE APPLICATION FOR EMPLOYMENT

LAST NAME	FIRST	MIDDLE	SOCIAL SECURITY NO.

PRESENT ADDRESS			TELEPHONE

CITY	STATE	ZIP	HEIGHT	WEIGHT

PERMANENT ADDRESS			TELEPHONE

CITY	STATE	ZIP	U.S. CITIZEN

REFERRED BY:

RELATIVE EMPLOYED BY COMPANY? NAME/DEPT.

IN EMERGENCY: NAME/ADDRESS	TELEPHONE

PERSONAL PHYSICIAN: NAME/ADDRESS	TELEPHONE

EDUCATION

	ELEMENTARY SCHOOL — NAME/LOCATION	YEARS ATTENDED	DATE GRADUATED
MIDDLE	HIGH SCHOOL — NAME/LOCATION	YEARS ATTENDED	GRADUATE? ☐ YES ☐ NO / WHEN
		MAJOR SUBJECT AREA	
	COLLEGE/TECHNICAL	YEARS ATTENDED	DATE GRADUATED
		MAJOR	DEGREE RECEIVED
FIRST	COLLEGE/TECHNICAL	YEARS ATTENDED	DATE GRADUATED
		MAJOR	DEGREE RECEIVED

MEMBER PROFESSIONAL ORGANIZATION	REGISTRATION NUMBER
MEMBER PROFESSIONAL ORGANIZATION	REGISTRATION NUMBER

SUBJECTS OF SPECIAL STUDY/RESEARCH

BUSINESS MACHINES YOU CAN OPERATE

LAST NAME

EMPLOYMENT RECORD
Include Military Experience If Applicable

EMPLOYER – NAME/ADDRESS	JOB TITLE		REF. CHK'D OFF. USE ONLY
	NAME OF SUPERVISOR		
	EMPLOYED FROM	TO	SALARY
	NAME WORKED UNDER		
	REASON FOR LEAVING		

EMPLOYER – NAME/ADDRESS	JOB TITLE		REF. CHK'D OFF. USE ONLY
	NAME OF SUPERVISOR		
	EMPLOYED FROM	TO	SALARY
	NAME WORKED UNDER		
	REASON FOR LEAVING		

EMPLOYER – NAME/ADDRESS	JOB TITLE		REF. CHK'D OFF. USE ONLY
	NAME OF SUPERVISOR		
	EMPLOYED FROM	TO	SALARY
	NAME WORKED UNDER		
	REASON FOR LEAVING		

EMPLOYER – NAME/ADDRESS	JOB TITLE		REF. CHK'D OFF. USE ONLY
	NAME OF SUPERVISOR		
	EMPLOYED FROM	TO	SALARY
	NAME WORKED UNDER		
	REASON FOR LEAVING		

REFERENCES

NAME	BUSINESS		REF. CHK'D OFF. USE ONLY
ADDRESS	YEARS KNOWN	FROM	TO
CITY	STATE		ZIP

NAME	BUSINESS		REF. CHK'D OFF. USE ONLY
ADDRESS	YEARS KNOWN	FROM	TO
CITY	STATE		ZIP

NAME	BUSINESS		REF. CHK'D OFF. USE ONLY
ADDRESS	YEARS KNOWN	FROM	TO
CITY	STATE		ZIP

(continued)

HIRING INFORMATION

Position Wanted			If Employed, May We Contact Present Employer?	How Much Notice Given To Last Employer?

Date Able To Start	Indicate Shifts You Can Work	Can You Work Weekends?	Distance From Home To Work	Method of Transportation

Salary Desired	Ever Apply To This Company Before?		Ever Collect Unemployment Compensation?	Ever Convicted of a Felony or Misdemeanor?
	Where?	When?		

I authorize investigation of all statements contained in this application. I understand that misrepresentation or omission of facts called for is cause for dismissal. Further, I understand and agree that my employment is for no definite period and may, regardless of payment of my wages and salary, be terminated at any time without previous notice.

DATE	APPLICANT'S SIGNATURE

DO NOT WRITE BELOW THIS LINE!

TELEPHONE REFERENCES CHECKED

REFERENCE 1

	Excellent	Good	Average	Fair	Poor
Integrity	☐	☐	☐	☐	☐
Neatness	☐	☐	☐	☐	☐
Conscientious	☐	☐	☐	☐	☐
Intelligence	☐	☐	☐	☐	☐
Skill in position	☐	☐	☐	☐	☐
Cooperation	☐	☐	☐	☐	☐
Absenteeism	☐ Average			☐ High	

REFERENCE 2

	Excellent	Good	Average	Fair	Poor
Integrity	☐	☐	☐	☐	☐
Neatness	☐	☐	☐	☐	☐
Conscientious	☐	☐	☐	☐	☐
Intelligence	☐	☐	☐	☐	☐
Skill in position	☐	☐	☐	☐	☐
Cooperation	☐	☐	☐	☐	☐
Absenteeism	☐ Average			☐ High	

REFERENCE 3

	Excellent	Good	Average	Fair	Poor
Integrity	☐	☐	☐	☐	☐
Neatness	☐	☐	☐	☐	☐
Conscientious	☐	☐	☐	☐	☐
Intelligence	☐	☐	☐	☐	☐
Skill in position	☐	☐	☐	☐	☐
Cooperation	☐	☐	☐	☐	☐
Absenteeism	☐ Average			☐ High	

REASON FOR SEPARATION	REASON FOR SEPARATION	REASON FOR SEPARATION
WOULD YOU RECOMMEND APPLICANT?	WOULD YOU RECOMMEND APPLICANT?	WOULD YOU RECOMMEND APPLICANT?
WOULD YOU RE-EMPLOY?	WOULD YOU RE-EMPLOY?	WOULD YOU RE-EMPLOY?

REMARKS

INTERVIEWED BY	DATE

REPORT FOR DUTY (DATE)	DEPARTMENT	POSITION	SALARY

My Generic Cover Letter

1.

2.

3.

4.
5.

6.

7.

My Focused Cover Letter

1.

2.

3.

4.

5.

6.

7.

CHAPTER -5

Preparing for the Interview

If I have eight hours to chop down a tree, I'll spend the first seven sharpening my ax.

Abraham Lincoln

Being good at something is only half the battle. The other half is mastering the art of self-presentation, positioning, and connecting.

Adele Scheele, author

Introduction

The moment of truth in the job-search process is the all-important interview. This chapter will help you prepare for it. This chapter will look at the planning process for the interview within the larger context of the job-search process. It will provide strategies and techniques that will help you to market your work experience, education, personal qualities, and skills, and to create an overall positive image. Creative problem solving and critical thinking will be highlighted as important abilities you will want to demonstrate during the interview. By preparing, getting organized, and learning verbal and nonverbal communication skills, you will stand out from the crowd. If you follow the strategies in this book, you *can* turn an interview into a job offer. People who learn to master the art of interviewing are often the same people who get promoted faster, make great presentations, have high self-esteem, and can transfer their skills to other jobs when necessary.

—

Learning Objectives

In Chapter 5, you will learn

• The purpose and importance of the interview.

• The importance of preparation as a key to success.

• The essential factors of the interview process.

• How to research likely questions and prepare good answers.

• How to plan a professional image.

• The importance of rehearsing the interview.

Your Chance to Shine

Finally! After all the effort, time, and work, you've landed an interview! You feel a surge of excitement and relief. You've been very busy, and everything you have done up to this point has been preparation for the interview. Planning, networking, researching, writing your resumé, composing specific cover letters, filling out an application, contacting references, and making telephone calls have all been done in order to get an interview. You have been "sharpening your saw," and your preparation will pay off.

Throughout the book, we have stressed that all job-search steps are interrelated and involve preparation, planning, and communication. The steps in the interview process are also linked to each other, with planning and communication as a foundation. Just as you have taken control of your job search so far, you can learn the strategies that will make you shine during each step of the job interview.

An effective interview is a combination of several factors and 10 steps. We'll cover the first three steps in this chapter—before the interview—and the remaining steps in Chapter 6.

The Importance and Purpose of the Interview

The first step in preparing for the interview is to realize its importance. In fact, it is the face-to-face interview that is most critical in getting the job you want. The best resumé, the most competent skills, and the most persuasive cover letter will not get you a job without an interview. The interview also creates a lasting impression that will influence your success on the job. A successful interview can help you command a higher salary, create higher expectations, and determine how well you will fit into the organization.

The purpose of the interview from the employer's point of view is to determine what skills you have and if these skills will match the needs of the company. The interviewer also wants to find out what kind of person you are, if you are a team player, and if you will benefit the company. The purpose of the interview from your point of view is to sell yourself. To do that, you need to show that your skills match the needs of the company, that you can make a contribution, and that you will fit into the company. In other words, you must convince the employer that you are the solution to the company's need or problem. In order to sell yourself, you must be well prepared and communicate your strengths and value.

An equally important purpose of the interview is to determine if the job is right for you. Through research, preparation, and asking questions you will be able to make a sound decision that fits with both your immediate and long-term career goals.

The Ten "R's" of Interviewing

Before the Interview:

1. Research.
2. Remember image.
3. Rehearse.

During the Interview:

4. Relax and overcome fear and anxiety.
5. Build rapport.
6. Review basic questions and answers.
7. Reinforce your skills and strengths.
8. Respond with questions.
9. Readjust and close.

After the Interview:

10. Reassess and follow up.

Step 1. Research

Research the Company

It is amazing that so few people investigate the company before an interview. Do your homework. You can't ask good questions or give really good answers if you don't have the necessary information. This is where your networking will pay off. Talk with your professional contacts. Someone may know an employee at the company where you're interviewing. Talk with anyone currently employed with the company or anyone who has previously worked with the company. Ask about problems, turnover rate of personnel, working environment, management style, and so on.

Preparation is the key to success. You should be aware of the company's products, services, size, divisions, age, recent activities, reputation, concerns or problems, new directions, and growth potential. Read as much as you can and get a corporate profile. Your local library can help you with this as well as with your search for articles about the company. Also check with your local chamber of commerce, or call the company directly and ask a receptionist to send information.

Other Resources Include:

Annual reports.

Catalogs, flyers, and newsletters.

Business Periodicals Index.

Standard and Poor's Corporation Records.

MacRae's Blue Book.

For each interview, create a company profile that includes the following information:

Company

- Job position.
- Plant size and location.
- Number of employees.
- Products.
- Sales.
- Profits.
- Concerns.
- Future plans.
- Job description of positions in question.

This information can be used in the interview to demonstrate you have done your homework. This degree of preparation indicates career maturity and ambition. For example:

I was interested to read an article in *The Wall Street Journal* about your employee incentive program.

or

Your annual report describes your impressive management training programs.

Research the Industry

Stay current on industry trends. You should be well versed in the industry you want to work in. Let's say you have just received your certificate as a medical technician. As a professional, you should know about key medical issues, new products, preventive treatment, and new trends in your field. Be prepared to talk about the industry. Put your network to use and talk with people in the field. Ask about the special problems, concerns, challenges, opportunities, and rewards involved. What is new in their field?

Your preparation will pay off when you are asked the question, Why do you think you will like being a medical technician? You will be able to give an informed and sensible answer. You have done your homework, shown interest, and taken the initiative.

Research the latest industry buzzwords—words that are used specially in the field. Take time to find out what they are in your area. You don't want to sound false and overprepared, but you should know the trends and language of your industry.

Common Words in Industry:

Computer
System design, database, modem.

Medical Records
Magnetic resonance imaging, record maintenance, record verification.

Legal
Brief, deposition, court calendar.

Management:
MBO, paradigm shifting, synergy, TQM, quality control.

Engineering
Surveying, drafting, environmental protection, design.

Electrical
Electricity generation, transmission.

Automotive
Computer diagnostics, scope analysis, preventive maintenance.

Research Details

Get organized and write down every detail. Begin by finding out the format for the interview. Write down the data on a sheet, leaving nothing to memory:

- Time of interview.
- Place of interview. (Find out exactly where it is: building, office.)
- Most convenient parking.
- People who will be there. (Check spelling, titles, and pronunciation.)

    Mr. John Ryan, Director of Marketing.

    Ms. Roberta Wess, Director of Public Affairs.

    Mr. Brian Weiss, Sales Director.

    Ms. Sandy Roland, Receptionist. (Remember, a receptionist or secretary may play the role of an unofficial screener. Everyone you meet may be asked their opinion of you.)

    Write everyone's name down on a notepad. People like to be recognized.
- Phone numbers of the main office and each of the above contacts (in case you are delayed).
- Directions to the company and the offices. Ask the best way to get to the interview. If the company is close, do a trial run and find out where the company and specific offices are, and how long it takes to get there.
- Length of the interview and plan for the day. (Is lunch included?)
- Material or information needed (samples of work applications, artwork, etc.).
- List of questions that may be asked.
- List of questions to ask.

Pack your briefcase with the previous information, plus the following:

- Several copies of your resumé.
- Research on the company.
- A pad of paper and two good pens.
- Reference letters.

Research Yourself

Review the section on self-assessment in Chapter 1. Make certain you have written out your strengths and abilities and your education and experiences, and that you have determined their value—both to you and to the employer. What have you done in previous jobs to demonstrate that you can solve problems, increase profits, and decrease costs?

Outline what you most want to stress in the interview. Review the section in Chapter 1 on writing your autobiography. Many interviewers probe into your early life in an attempt to find out the character or habits you formed early. What life experiences did you have that demonstrated positive qualities? Later in this chapter, you will learn how to connect your skills and accomplishments with the needs of the job. In the next chapter, you will learn how to build rapport. Researching yourself is good preparation for both of these important areas.

Take some time to review your resumé again, too. Remind yourself of the skills you've demonstrated.

Research Questions

Prepare questions that you think the interviewer will ask based upon the job description and your research about the company. Collect other questions from people in your network. Your contacts in the same field or at similar companies will be able to provide you with questions you are likely to be asked. You can expect questions concerning your education, job skills, work experience, personality, whether you are a team player, and how you deal with stress. The most common questions fall into the categories below.

Work Experience

What do you enjoy most (or least) about your present job?

What were your major accomplishments in each of your jobs?

Describe your technical skills.

Explain specific duties or a typical day on the job.

Describe the best supervisor you ever had. Describe the worst.

What have been the biggest failures or frustrations in your professional life?

Why do you want to leave your current job?

Educational Background and Training

Why did you decide to go to college? How well did you do?

What did your major courses prepare you to do?

Did you work while going to school?

What leadership role did you demonstrate in school activities?

Are you willing to get advanced training?

Character and Personality Traits

Tell me about yourself.

What are your major strengths? Your major weakness?

What causes you to lose your temper?

Have you ever had to deal with an angry customer? How did you handle that person?

How do you deal with stress?

Decision-Making and Problem-Solving Abilities

Describe a problem that you solved that you were proud of.

What decision do you most regret making?

What problems do you think you could help us solve?

Here's a typical work problem. How would you solve it?

Here's a typical decision that you may make on this job. What process would you go through to make a sound decision?

In this job, there are a lot of pressures to meet deadlines. If you are given three top priorities, how would you determine which to accomplish first? (They may give you examples such as: The computer is down, a colleague wants to talk about personal problems, and a disgruntled customer is waiting to see you.)

What process do you go through to make important decisions?

What is the worst problem you ever had to solve?

Career Goals

Where do you want to be professionally five years from now? What do you see yourself doing to make yourself more effective?

What are your long-term career goals?

Why do you want this job?

Why do you think you're the best person for this job?

How do you feel about traveling, relocating, or learning new skills?

What attracted you to this company?

Why should we hire you? What can you do that will benefit the company most?

If you could create your ideal job, what would it be?

Teamwork

What types of people do you like to work with?

What types of people do you find difficult?

Describe a team project you were involved in.

Confident Answers to Tough Questions

Preparation will help you answer even tough questions. You will want to use your own style and give appropriate examples and personal accomplishments. You want to be prepared, rehearsed, and confident, but your answers shouldn't sound glib or pat. Use the answers below only as a guide. Sincerity is important in an interview.

Keep in mind that you want to listen for the *intent* of the question. Sometimes there is a hidden meaning beneath the surface of a question.

Tell me about yourself.

This question is often designed to help break the ice, to get you talking freely about yourself, to determine what you consider to be important about your life, and to see if you ramble at such an open-ended question.

Be prepared. Outline the main areas of your life that are most relevant to the job. Choose one personality characteristic that you want to focus on. You may want to highlight your hardworking nature and include an example:

> I started working when I was 12. I had a paper route and also worked in my parent's business after school and on weekends. I put my heart into what I do and am not concerned about quitting at 5:00. I have worked late many evenings and weekends to complete a project that I am proud of.

EXERCISE 5.1   Tell Me about Yourself

Since this is one of the most common interview questions, take some time to outline your response in the space below.

_____

_____

_____

_____

_____

_____

_____

_____

_____

Why do you want to leave your current job?

The standard answer is that you are ready for a new challenge, or you want to develop your skills and use all your capabilities. You may want to expand your answer to include your present situation. Say, for example, that your company has cut back on promotions due to tough times. You might respond:

> When I accepted this position last year, I understood that I would be promoted within a year if my performance reviews were acceptable. I have received outstanding reviews, demonstrated my abilities, and have a solid track record of producing results. However, because of cutbacks and reorganization, the company has decided not to expand our department, and a promotion will not be possible for at least another year. It has been a difficult decision, but I believe it is time to find a company where I can make a real contribution in a position that I am qualified for.

What can you contribute to this company?

This type of question is designed to see if you have done your homework on the company and to determine if you are just after any job or if you have specific skills that you think can benefit the company. You will want to take one point in the job description and highlight how your skills would meet these current needs. For example:

> You have mentioned that you want to improve customer relations in this office. This is an area that I have a real interest in and have excelled in. I developed the first guidelines for customer relations while I was an intern at Bancroft. I also have received several letters from satisfied customers for putting extra effort into solving their concerns. I have called customers on my own time if I cannot reach them during business hours. I believe that customer service is the heart of a business. A little extra time and concern really pays off.

What kind of people annoy you most?

Questions like this one, or: What makes you angry? or: What do you worry about? can give you the impression that the interviewer wants to chat. Actually, these types of questions are designed to determine if you are a team player, like diversity, and can handle stress. Don't reveal your personal life or make a confession. Maintain a professional demeanor at all times. It is best to keep your answer focused on how you handle difficult people, tension, conflict, or pet peeves on the job. For example:

> I am a professional and am responsible for my behavior. I respond in a calm manner even to angry people. I focus on the problem and don't let people cause me to lose sight of finding a solution. I work well with a variety of people and see diversity as an important element in working teams. My ability to work well with a variety of people is one strength that has helped me in my career.

I see you have worked with Wes Neilson? Did you enjoy this experience?

Be careful about giving a negative response even if the interviewer implies that a person is difficult to work with. Standard advice is to never bad-mouth anyone during an interview. You might say, "Oh, so you know Wes. I learned a lot working with him. Did you work with him too?"

What are your greatest strengths (or personal qualities)?

You might be tempted to start rattling off a list of virtues. Don't. Select a few key points and explain how you have demonstrated them. For example:

> I am persistent and take initiative. I worked full time but finished my degree by going to school three or four nights a week for several years. In addition, I took the initiative with my marketing club to put together a leadership conference. I work well on my own and don't have to be shown every little detail.

Review the list of most desirable personal characteristics and determine what experiences you want to highlight.

What are your greatest weaknesses or shortcomings?

You can turn this around and make the question and the weakness work for you. Again, look at the list of personal qualities, and don't make your answer sound flip or insincere. Give this question some real thought.

> Some people have called me a perfectionist. I am a stickler for details and must admit that I have worked nights and weekends to make certain all project details were completed. I am persistent and must take pride in my work. I have learned, however, to pace myself, delegate minor details, and make certain they are completed, but I have learned not to do it all myself.

You might also indicate what you are doing to overcome a weakness. "I am taking a course on time management and it is helping me be more efficient and organized."

Answer all questions honestly, but stress the positive, not the negative.

What are your weaknesses?

Almost everyone has certain weaknesses, liabilities, or handicaps. An interviewer may not voice a concern out loud but may wonder if a particular factor would affect your ability to perform or fit into the company. It is best to face any area that others might see as a liability and turn it into an asset. What are some perceived liabilities that an interviewer may have about you? Add to the following list.

Common Liabilities Cited by Employers

Too young.

Too old.

Changes jobs too frequently.

Change of careers.

No work experience.

Unemployed.

Woman applying in a traditionally male field.

Physically handicapped.

EXERCISE 5.2   Turning a Weakness into an Asset

Review the above list of perceived liabilities and turn each into an asset. For example:

Perceived Liability	Positive Asset
Too young	Ability to learn quickly, flexibility, enthusiasm, and high energy.
Too old	Maturity, good judgment, experience, and good work ethic.

How have you handled a major disappointment in your life?

You can use the same pattern for questions that ask about an important decision that you have had to make, how you handled a major challenge in your job, or how you have handled a major disappointment. Always look at these as two-part questions. First tell the process and then give an example. Look over your list of personal qualities and decide how to build an example around one of the qualities you possess. For example:

I was very disappointed that I was turned down for college football. I had excelled in high school and spent the summer in training. But I view disappointments as stepping stones, not barriers. I always ask myself what I can learn from a situation and how I can benefit from it. I looked for other doors to open. After getting over my disappointment, I joined the swimming team and as a result earned a scholarship and made wonderful friends. Resiliency and a positive attitude have seen me through many disappointments.

When was the last time you worked on a team project? What did you accomplish?

The purpose of this type of question is to determine if you are a team player and can work well with others to achieve the mission of the organization. (During your research of the company, you should have called and obtained a copy of the organization's mission statement.) In the new workplace, employees are increasingly working in self-managed teams. Since there is an increased emphasis on teamwork, employers want to hire self-starters who are team players with effective interpersonal communication skills. Your answer should include knowledge of other departments and examples of how you have worked as a team member to accomplish results. Give examples of how you have demonstrated creative problem solving, critical thinking, and listening skill.

What is the worst job you've ever had?

The interviewer is trying to get at your sense of values, what you consider menial, the appreciation of the whole process, and if you have failed to omit a job on your resumé. (Some people leave out jobs they consider unpleasant or irrelevant.) You will want to assure the interviewer that even part-time, low-level jobs have been valuable. You have learned the importance of hard work, time management, working with others, and so forth. You know the importance of the entire job process, have empathy for workers who perform all types of tasks, and see the value of each component in the completed product.

Describe a difficult problem you had to solve.

Don't focus so much on the problem as on the process. Employers are interested in problem-solving ability and whether you can use critical thinking skills and creativity to solve problems and make decisions. You might say:

> I take a step-by-step approach. First, I state the problem clearly and in writing. I look for the real issues involved and who is affected, and determine if I can solve the problem by myself. Next, I gather information on the problem, talk to others about similar situations, and brainstorm a list of possible solutions. Third, I weigh and project the probable consequences for the top solutions.

Continue with this process and give an example:

> When I was hired as a new sales rep, sales were down and morale was poor. I had a problem with customers' perception of service. I increased my service line, installed a hot line where complaints could be handled, and increased my contacts with each contractor. The results were amazing. We increased our sales by 25 percent and, just as important, evaluations showed that our customers were delighted by our new service.

Describe the worst boss you ever had.

Questions regarding your previous bosses, how you handle criticism, or what your boss or references would say about you are designed to catch you off guard and see if you blame others or are a negative person. Always be positive, and keep this answer short. You might say that one boss was a perfectionist and outspoken. Another had personality problems, but you worked with her very well and appreciated knowing where you stood at all times. You learned to follow through on even tiny details, and as a result you take enormous pride in your work. This is one of those, "Will this person fit in?" questions. Variations include, "What don't you like about your boss?" "How do you handle disagreements with your boss?" "Can we call your references?" The same rule applies. Stay positive. No one wants a troublemaker, someone who is thin-skinned, or someone who has something to hide.

Always be honest, but don't volunteer information that hasn't been asked. Stay focused on the positive. Avoid using words such as *can't* or *dislike*.

Don't send reference letters unless they are asked for, then say, "Please feel free to contact my references. I've alerted them that you may be calling."

How do you handle stress?

You want to demonstrate that you can deal with stress effectively. Rather than react to stress, you work to eliminate the causes of stress, and you plan and solve problems before they become crises. No employer wants to hire a hothead or someone who blows up or is petty with customers or co-workers. Nor do employers want employees who consistently ignore problems until they become serious, stressful matters.
You might say:

> I transform stress into positive energy. I like the excitement of a busy day, but I don't let tensions build. I find that if I am well organized, break tasks down, set priorities, and have a vision of the final project, I can stay on track and not feel overwhelmed. I plan my work and solve problems as they arise so that crises don't occur. I also jog or walk every day to get rid of stress. It helps me to keep from overreacting or panicking about deadlines.

Step 2. Remember Image

Create a Polished, Professional Image

Prepare for the interview by giving thought to the professional image you want to project. Your clothes, hair, and body language make a statement about you. (Tips for creating a positive first impression will be discussed further in Chapter 6.)

You should project the image of being neat, conservative, and clean. Dressing for a job interview is not just a matter of personal opinion or style. It is actually a science, based on research involving thousands of professionals. Although you may not like the idea, dressing for an interview is essentially wearing an appropriate uniform. You do not want to detract from your message, but rather use clothing to enhance your professional image. John Molloy, in his best selling book, *Dress for Success,* stresses the importance of looking professional and offers guidelines that are still well accepted by professionals. Of course, there are exceptions to the rules, such as jobs in art fields or in entertainment, but you should only dress differently if you know your supervisor and interviewers will be dressed in a similar manner.

Projecting a professional, businesslike appearance is very important. Remember that a job interview is not a social event. However, underdressing tends to be more of a problem. Short-sleeved dresses and shirts, casual and sloppy clothes are unacceptable. In general, dressing for the job higher than the one you are applying for is a good rule of thumb. Even if you are interviewing for a job that allows casual dress (park ranger, outdoor recreation job, geology field work), you should wear a suit for the interview.

The following guidelines are appropriate for men and women who want to project a positive and professional image.

Dress for Career Success

Guidelines for Men

Suit: Dress in a conservative, tailored, good quality, dark blue, gray, or muted pin-striped suit. Don't wear bold plaids or stripes.

Shirt: Wear a good quality, white or pale blue, button-down shirt that is clean and pressed. Cuffs should show no more than 1/2 inch. Make certain the shirt fits. A tight collar is very uncomfortable. Don't wear faddish styles or cheap fabrics.

Tie: Wear a conservative, good quality tie that complements your suit. Avoid faddish prints, loud colors, bold patterns, clip-ons or bow ties.

Socks: Socks should be calf-length and match your suit and shoes.

Shoes: Wear polished, laced, dress or slip-on shoes in black or brown. Don't wear loafers, faddish styles, scuffed heels, or light colors.

Watch and jewelry: Wear a conservative watch. Don't wear jewelry except for a wedding band or a class ring. Don't wear pins or jewelry that are religious or affiliated with societies or organizations.

Hair: Hair should be neat, styled, and fairly short. Don't wear faddish cuts.

Grooming: Grooming should be impeccable. Eyeglasses should be spotless; fingernails should be clean and trimmed. No heavy aftershave or cologne.

Guidelines for Women

Suit: Wear a good quality, conservative, dark suit that is at or just below the knee. A conservative dress with a jacket is the next best choice, but a suit is preferred. Blue, gray, beige, or tan are preferred colors. Don't wear faddish styles. (Never wear a pant suit.)

Blouse: Wear a good quality, simple blouse. Avoid tight or low cut blouses. Wear a color that complements you.

Stockings: Wear beige, tan, or neutral hose. (Keep an extra pair in your briefcase.)

Shoes: Wear dark, two-inch or less, closed heels. Shoes should be polished.

Watch and jewelry: Wear a conservative watch. Wear small earrings and no more than two simple rings. Don't wear dangling earrings or evening jewelry. Less is best.

Hair: Wear a simple and becoming style that is clean and neat. Avoid fads and long, curly, or fussy styles.

Grooming: You want to project a clean, neat, and professional image. Eyeglasses should be spotless. Avoid heavy makeup. Don't use perfume, or use only a tiny amount. Nail polish should be clear or light, and nails should be trimmed neatly.

Briefcase:

Both men and women should carry a good attaché case. This can carry a good pen, backup pens and pencils, a legal pad, breath mints, a comb or brush, extra copies of your resumé, and other important material. The case can also double as a purse for a woman, or a small purse can fit inside the attaché case. Keep the essentials together. You don't want to fumble when you are shaking hands. You want to look professional, simple, neat, and confident.

You may be thinking that these guidelines are too rigid and confining. After all, shouldn't a company be more concerned with your skills and accomplishments? Yes, but your clothes and style make a statement, and image is important to all companies. No employer wants to hire someone who is sloppy and poorly groomed or who looks as if he or she were going out for the evening. The above guidelines will help you project a professional image in almost all business interviewing situations. It is often the little things that make a difference in a successful interview. This is not the time to have a chip on your shoulders that says, "I'll dress any way I like." You will have the competitive edge if you present yourself in a neat, conservative, and professional way. Dress any way you want on your own time. Dress professionally and appropriately when at work.

Pull together one really great-looking outfit. Look through your closet for clothes that you can use to build an outfit around. Do you have a great blouse or shirt, tie, scarf, or shoes? You probably know at least one friend who likes to shop and is aware of how important a professional look is. Ask this friend for advice or if you can borrow clothes if necessary. This is not the time to go for fads or far-out costumes. You want to pull together one or two good business outfits. Don't overlook consignment shops or second-hand stores. Often they have expensive, timeless suits, silk shirts, and classic accessories at a fraction of their original price. Be careful to avoid clothes that are too worn or out of style, however.

Step 3. Rehearse

Any new skill requires practice. Rehearse your presentation on a tape recorder, on a video, and with one of your networking contacts. Critique yourself and request feedback from others. How do you come across? Feeling prepared helps you relax and be yourself. The more you practice, adjust, and rehearse, the more comfortable and easy it will be to interview. You don't want to sound canned, but relaxed, natural, and confident. Role-playing will help you practice and also help you reduce fear and anxiety.

EXERCISE 5.4   Practice Your Interviewing Skills

You don't become good at any skill by just reading about it; you need to actually practice. Your interviewing skills will improve through practice and role-playing. Review the questions and suggested answers in this chapter. Add to the list and modify the answers to fit your style and experience.

Task 1: Form triads. Person A is the interviewer, person B is the interviewee, and person C is the observer. Form about six questions to ask each other. The observer takes notes on the responses.

Questions to ask   **Main points you want to make**

_____

Task 2: Take turns playing each role.
Write out your observations.

Observations as the interviewer:

_____

Observations as the interviewee:

_____

Observer's notes:

_____

Though every interview is different, the positive habits and techniques you've learned in this chapter will prepare you for almost any interview situation. By researching the company, the field, and yourself; preparing questions and answers; learning verbal and nonverbal communication; creating a professional image; and practicing, you are now ready to shine during the actual interview. In Chapter 6, you will learn how to channel fear into focused energy, how to build rapport, and how to readjust and close an interview. Both chapters stress the importance of connecting your skills and strengths to the needs of the company.

THE BENEFIT FACTOR:
Sell Yourself

The Benefit Factor

The job interview is really a sales job. You are there to sell yourself and your unique combination of qualities and skills to an employer. Marketing any product is based upon need and benefit. Most people don't buy a product unless they have a need or want to solve a problem. Therefore, your preparation for the interview should focus on the company's needs and problems and how you can add value to the company.

The work you did earlier in this book will provide the framework for the interview. The exercises and journal entries were not just interesting side trips into self-reflection, but designed to help you market and sell yourself. You have invested the time necessary to assess what you want to do, what fits your current situation, and what you are good at. You have assessed your skills, education, job experience, and goals. You have assessed and practiced your problem-solving and creative decision-making skills. You have analyzed various positions in numerous companies and assessed how your skills relate to these jobs. Your resumé demonstrates that you are capable of performing the job by highlighting experience, education, and skills. Your cover letter shows how your skills and abilities relate to the specific job being offered and indicate your enthusiasm, problem-solving abilities, and willingness to succeed. You have succeeded in getting an interview. Now you can use all this information to put your best foot forward and clearly show the benefit connection.

The question that should be running through your head while you are preparing for the interview is, What can I do to make the company more profitable? Companies are concerned about saving money and producing more and better services or products. Whenever possible, demonstrate to potential employers how you have saved time and money, or increased production in previous jobs. Follow this outline to apply the benefit connection:

> **Accomplishment:** Designed and implemented a computerized accounting system.
>
> **Skills and personal qualities used:** Formal training, knowledge, and experience in IBM and MacIntosh computers. Ability to train staff of five people to implement new system. Good communication skills and organization skills.
>
> **Benefit:** Reduced errors, saved time, decreased spending by 5 percent.
>
> **Benefit to company:** Demonstrated the ability to train staff and implement a new system that increased production by 20 percent.

THE SKILLED WORKFORCE

Key: Training and Education

The earning gap is widening between those with marketable skills and those without. Statistics indicate that the average college-educated man between the ages of 24 and 34 earns $40,000. The average college-educated woman earns $30,000. The average man of the same age who has not earned a high school diploma earns $18,200, and the average woman earns $14,500. Just think, one college graduate earns more than two people who didn't graduate from high school. The gulf between high earners and low earners is the largest in history and is distinctly linked to those with marketable skills and those without. The major reason for this gap is the decline of mass-production jobs and an increase in white-collar and technical jobs.

Workplace Trends

The new economy and work rules demand that employees receive training and education beyond high school. Learning new skills is essential for job success. Besides technical schools, local community colleges are providing certificates and training in computers, equipment repair, health care, waste management, and financial planning. Every employee must reinvent him- or herself with up-to-date skills. In addition, employers want to hire well-rounded people who have positive work habits and good personal qualities. Job security will come not from a company, but from maintaining a portfolio of marketable technical and personal skills.

Career Strategies: Be a lifelong learner and continually add technical and human relations skills to your job.

HITTING THE WALL

Scaling the Wall

You've put a lot of time into reflection, preparing your database, reviewing your achievements, researching careers and jobs, networking, preparing and sending out a great resumé and cover letter, and linking your achievements with the needs of the company. Now you want action!

It is easy to lose patience with details at this stage of the job search. You question whether you can really prepare for an interview and if it will do any good to try and research questions. You may not feel inspired to practice. You just want to jump in and start interviewing. Realize that this impatience is normal but that it is essential to overcome it and keep on track with your job search. Preparation is a major factor in the success of your job interview.

Scaling the Wall

Preparation is the key to many successes in life. Keep focused on your goals and the details that are critical to the preparation process. Set daily priorities. Assess your progress by measuring tangible results. Keep a to-do list as part of your pre-interview preparation strategies.

To-Do List

Activity	Date	Result
1. Research the company.		
2. Research the industry.		
3. Research all details of the interview.		
4. Research yourself.		
5. Research interview questions.		
6. Prepare wardrobe.		
7. Practice interviewing.		

The Knockout Factor

- Not preparing or researching for the interview.
- Not researching the company.
- Not researching the industry.
- Not researching the details of the interview.
- Not researching yourself.
- Not researching interview questions
- Dressing inappropriately or unprofessionally.
- Not rehearsing.

The Success Factor

- Doing your homework and being prepared.
- Researching the company.
- Researching the industry.
- Researching all details of the interview.
- Researching yourself.
- Researching interview questions.
- Dressing professionally and appropriately.
- Rehearsing until you are comfortable.

PROBLEM SOLVING AT WORK

Problem Solving

Vicky graduated with an Associate of Arts degree from a well-known career school. She has an impressive array of computer and office skills and has developed good work habits. She is hardworking, personable, and has a positive attitude.

Vicky very much wants a career as an executive secretary and has prepared for the interview. She researched the company and the industry. She has written down all the details concerning the interview and knows the name and title of the people who will be interviewing her. She has thought through her experiences, strengths, weaknesses, and values, and reviewed her database. Vicky has researched questions and prepared a list of sample answers. She has practiced interviewing and feels prepared. The only problem is deciding what to wear. Vicky has worked as a fashion model and loves to wear the latest fashions. She doesn't own a suit and feels that corporate dressing is boring. She wants to make her own fashion statement and likes leather mini skirts, long straight hair, and lots of jewelry.

Here's how Vicky used creative problem solving to explore solutions and critical thinking to make her decision.

She will be interviewing for a top secretarial job in a large conservative corporation.

1. Have I clearly stated the problems? Should I dress in a conservative suit or wear the latest in fashion?

> **Define problem:** I want to reflect a professional image but also look stylish.
> **What:** What can I wear that will clearly reflect a professional look?
> **Who:** Who will be interviewing me? For whom would I be working?
> **When:** When do I need to start pulling together a professional outfit?
> **Where:** Where do I go to get a professional outfit?

2. Do I have enough information? Do I have all the information I need to make a decision? Have I researched how important a professional image is to this job? Have I gathered information concerning the corporate dress and cultural norms of the company?

3. Can I make the decision by myself? What resources are available to help me make a better decision? Have I talked with a career counselor, a fashion consultant, or my instructors?

4. Have I brainstormed alternatives? Have I creatively explored alternatives? Could I create a professional look with my own style? Could I save high fashion for the weekends?

5. Have I looked at likely consequences? If I create a professional, conservative image will I increase my chances of getting a job? What other consequences might occur if I wear an unprofessional outfit?

6. Have I identified all the resources and tools needed? Have I researched the resources available? Am I aware of classes, career centers, and job search books that would help me develop a more professional business look? Am I willing to acquire the additional skills, tools, and wardrobe to be successful?

7. Have I developed and implemented an action plan? Have I designed an action plan that will help me make sound decisions?

8. Have I identified the best solution and done everything possible to ensure success? Have I made a decision using critical thinking and creativity? Am I committed to making the decision a success?

9. Have I assessed the results? Have I evaluated my decision to see if it is working? Have I assessed the results of my plan and how they fit with my goals?

10. Have I modified the plan, if necessary? What adjustments could I make that would make my decision more successful?

Pre-Interview Strategies

- Prepare for the interview.
- Research the company.
- Research the industry.
- Research details.
- Research yourself.
- Research interview questions.
- Research and project a professional image.
- Rehearse your presentation.

Pre-Interview Checklist   Yes   No

1. Have you reviewed the pre-interview process?
Have you
    Remembered image?
    Rehearsed interview?

2. Have you completed the necessary research?
Including
    Company?
    Industry?
    Details?
    Yourself?
    Questions?

3. Have you prepared questions?
Are they
    Well thought out?
    Sincere?
    Direct?
    Skill-and achievement-oriented?

4. Have you considered the importance of image?
Including
    Dress?
    Hair?
    Cleanliness?
    Overall image?

5. Have you rehearsed the interview?
Including
    Questions?
    Answers?
    Appearance and presence?

The Interview

Introduction

Throughout this book, preparation has been stressed as a key factor in the success of the job-search process. Chapter 5 covered the importance of preparing for the interview. If you have researched the company, matched your skills with the company's needs, planned a professional image, developed questions, and rehearsed, you have done much to ensure a successful interview. Equally important to the interview is the ability to concentrate, be fully present, and communicate your strengths and values. Your image, sense of presence, and skill in responding to the questions will make the difference in selling yourself. In this chapter, we will discuss what to do during an interview: how to relax and channel stress into a positive force, make a positive and lasting first impression, build rapport, stress your strengths and reinforce your skills, ask questions, and readjust and close the interview. You will learn to manage the interview process to achieve the results you want.

—

Learning Objectives

In Chapter 6, you will learn

- How to relax and overcome fear and anxiety.

- The importance of the first impression.

- How to build rapport and respect.

- How to conduct a successful lunch or dinner interview.

- How to listen and ask thoughtful questions.

- The importance of personal qualities.

- How to clearly show how your skills will benefit the company.

- What an employer really wants in an employee.

- How to readjust and close an interview.

In Chapter 5, the three steps of preparing for the interview process were explained:

1. Research.
2. Remember image.
3. Rehearse.

Now that you have fully prepared, what can you do during and after the interview to ensure success? The answer is found in steps 4–10 of the interview process.

Evaluation: A Closer Look

Knowing what to expect can reduce fear of the unknown. Most companies use an evaluation sheet to rate applicants during the interview. The typical evaluation system generally covers the following areas:

- **Competence**

Competence includes work experience, knowledge of the field, achievements, and grades. The following is an example of a good response to a question concerning competency:

> I earned a 3.2 GPA while working part-time, being very involved in the accounting club, and volunteering for the chamber of commerce. My internship, work experience, and volunteer experience at the chamber of commerce were just as valuable as my formal education. I learned a great deal about accounting and teamwork and made many valuable contacts in my field.

- **Clearly defined career goals**

Employers want to be sure that you have a clear sense of where you are going and that you know what you want to do. The following is an example of a good response to demonstrating that you have career maturity:

> Since I have been around small business all my life, I have always been interested in all aspects of business. In high school, I took an accounting class and knew this was what I wanted to do. I started helping my Dad with his books. I chose Brady Business School because it has a good accounting department. There is no doubt that accounting is the field I want to be in.

- **Communication**

Since communication is such an important job skill, employers are interested in how well you speak. Some interview evaluation forms have categories for speaking in an articulate, clear, concise, and logical manner.

> My Dad owned his own business, so I was involved in business for as long as I can remember. I did stock work in the summers and helped with marketing and sales. I never saw any job as boring or menial. I wanted to learn every aspect of our business.

- **Enthusiasm and a positive attitude**

A positive attitude is one of the most important factors in job success. Employers are looking for someone who shows enthusiasm and interest and who has an upbeat outlook.

> I was very interested in reading about your overseas branch office. I took French and Spanish in high school and have always loved different cultures. Your training program also emphasizes the opportunities for international trade. I am very interested in learning new skills so that I can grow with the company.

- **Leadership**

Since hiring is a big investment, many companies want to hire employees who have leadership potential.

> I was vice president of the accounting club and was instrumental in starting the first mentor program for freshmen. This resulted in a 14 percent increase in the retention rate of freshmen. I would love to be involved, in any way, with programs designed to retain employees.

- **Personal qualities**

Employees are very interested in personal qualities, such as honesty, integrity, commitment, dependability, maturity, responsibility, and fairness.

> I was the oldest of four children, and both my parents had jobs that required travel. I learned to be responsible, hardworking, and dependable. I also tried to set a good example for my younger brothers and sisters. I wanted them to look up to me and to teach them good values. One time when I was 14, we had all just gotten home from grocery shopping. I discovered that the clerk had undercharged me. We all walked back to give the clerk the $5.00 that we owed.

- **Problem solving**

Analytical ability and logical inquiry are important to employers. Indicate how you use critical thinking to make decisions and solve problems.

> I have good business judgement and common sense. Recently I was responsible for locking up the store at night, and the power went out on one of the machines. I went through a logical process of solving the problem. I found the manual and had the power restored.

- **Overall appearance**

Your overall appearance makes a big first impression. If you are neat, clean, and professionally dressed, and if you walk and talk in a confident manner, you will create a professional overall image. Use direct eye contact, a confident, clear voice, and effective communication.

Step 4. Relax

Most people feel a bit nervous and apprehensive before they go to a job interview. For some people, however, the interview stage causes such extreme fear that they experience severe anxiety and apprehension. They are so stressed out that they either become paralyzed and tongue-tied or nervously talk themselves right out of a job. Companies want confident and polished employees who can perform even in stressful situations and can communicate effectively. If you stammer, shake, and appear nervous, chances are you won't be hired.

It is normal to experience some jitters. After all, instead of dealing with paper and phones, the interview calls on you to face a real person and sell yourself. In a sense, you are on stage. You are the center of attention, and all eyes are on you to see if you fit into the organization. This can cause mild to severe stage fright. Interviewing is a lot like public speaking, causing similar types of stress. Stress, however, can give you a rush of energy. Many performers and athletes say that it is the controlled stress that makes for an outstanding performance. Preparation is the key! When you are well prepared, you feel more confident and in control.

Being well prepared for the interview will help you channel and reduce the stress and will greatly increase your chances of success.

You also have to overcome your fear of speaking and of being rejected. Effective communication skills are vital, not only in the interview, but throughout your career. The higher up you go in an organization, the more you will need to make presentations, interview others, and chair meetings. Imagery, positive self-talk, and relaxation techniques can make a big difference in learning to channel stress, fear, and stage fright. You want to give your best performance as you communicate your strengths and value.

Top athletes know that they can improve their performance when they manage anxiety and stress. Sports psychology helps them improve their focus and concentration through relaxation, imagery, and positive self-talk. You can use the same techniques for improving your performance during your job search.

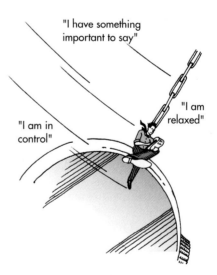

Relaxation

First learn how to relax and quiet your mind. Find a quiet place. Sit with your legs uncrossed and your arms at your side. Take several deep, slow breaths and exhale slowly. Close your eyes and relax your entire body. Drop your shoulders, roll your head, and breathe all the tension from your body. Clear your mind of all chatter and concentrate on deep breathing. Feel your muscles relax and your body grow heavy. Drop your jaws and shoulders. As your breathing becomes slower and deeper, you will become more relaxed and centered. Do this relaxation technique several times before your interview.

Imagery

Clearly visualize yourself being interviewed. Imagine every detail of the interview. See yourself looking and feeling confident and polished. Picture yourself speaking calmly and answering all questions with a graceful and convincing style. You are self-assured and making an impact on the employer. Visualize yourself relaxed and fully in the present. You are focused on the questions and communicating directly with the other person. Imagine a positive outcome.

Positive Self-talk

People who suffer from anxiety and stage fright often talk themselves into a state of panic. This negative talk is often followed by shallow breathing, sweaty palms, butterflies, and more negative self-talk. You may begin to question your sense of worth. You can stop this cycle of negativity and create a cycle of success. You do have control over your thoughts, and self-talk and can reprogram your mind for success. By jotting down a few of the negative sayings that flit through your mind, you'll become more aware of ways in which you are creating your own fear and anxiety. The following examples show how you can reprogram your mind by using positive self-talk or affirmations. Set goals, practice positive habits, and increase your skills. Your self-esteem will improve, and you will feel more confident and competent.

Stress-Provoking Talk	Stress-Reducing Talk
I'll never get a job.	I will get a job.
I am so nervous.	I am confident and well prepared.
Other people are better than me.	I have many skills and qualities.
I just want this to be over.	It is a pleasure to relate my strengths and value to the company.
I dread interviews.	I will smile, relax, and enjoy this.

Step 5. Build Rapport

Since the decision to hire someone often comes down to the simple factor of being likable (the resumé screens out candidates who are not qualified), it is important to build rapport with the interviewer. Rapport is the ability to find common ground with another person. People who are good at building rapport have a way of making others feel comfortable and good about themselves. They are good at reading nonverbal cues and adjusting their communication to achieve real understanding. They know how to build rapport in a sincere and genuine manner. Whether or not rapport is established generally depends on the first few minutes of contact.

First Impressions

First impressions are extremely important and difficult to change. Studies indicate that interviewers make up their minds quickly about a job candidate. It is during the first minute or two that the interviewer makes an initial decision about how well you would fit into the company. The first few minutes also set the tone for the entire interview. From the time you walk in the door, judgments are made about your personality, character, competency, and style. Your appearance communicates a great deal about you.

This initial impression is based on dress, eye contact, body language, posture, and verbal communication. Nonverbal communication can influence the first impression even more than words.

Body Language

Many job searchers spend hours finding just the right verbal response and forget about the importance of nonverbal communication. Body language carries over 90 percent of the meaning you are trying to convey. Gestures, body stance, facial expressions, clothes, hairstyle, jewelry, walk, and posture all work together to create an image. Assess your body language:

Do you have direct eye contact without staring?

Are your facial expressions warm, sincere, and expressive?

Are your gestures relaxed and natural, or do they seem forced?

Do you walk confidently and sit tall?

You can say all the right words, but if your body language or tone is incongruent or out of sync, people will usually believe your body language and tone of voice. You don't want to give a double message. For example, a candidate may be interviewing for a job and talk about the importance of teamwork and sensitivity and yet be sitting in an aloof manner, using little eye contact, and speaking in a flat tone of voice. The disparity will be noted and questioned.

Assess your consistency. You may want to videotape yourself and have a good friend watch it with you. Or ask several people to give you their honest feedback. Ask yourself the following:

Do you come across to others as honest and forthright?

Do people tend to trust you?

Take note of your tone of voice, body language, and words. Are they consistent?

Do you come across as a good listener?

Are you misunderstood often?

The purpose of the building-rapport stage is to put you at ease. The interviewer wants to get a picture of the real person behind the resumé.

The question being asked during this stage is, Are you poised, confident, and professional looking? Your challenge is to present a professional and polished first impression, or the interview is essentially over.

A Confident Image

Use positive body language (see below), and walk tall with your shoulders back and your head high. Maintain direct and frequent eye contact. Smile and show warmth and attentiveness. Say, "Hello, I'm John McAllen (first name and last name). It's a pleasure to meet you." Use a firm, yet gentle, handshake. Nothing is a bigger turnoff than a limp handshake. Relax while sitting straight. Don't fidget or engage in nervous habits such as playing with your hair, keys, coins, or pen. Sit relaxed, but with your spine straight and your shoulders back.

Practice the five essential habits for projecting a confident image and creating a positive first impression:

1. Smile.
2. Maintain direct eye contact.
3. Repeat the person's name.
4. Give a firm handshake.
5. Walk and sit tall, straight, and relaxed.

Casual Conversation

Be prepared to talk about yourself. A typical question is *Tell me about yourself*, as we saw in Chapter 5. Don't start with the story of your life. Instead, choose a recent job experience and relate your achievements. For example:

> I just graduated from Benson Business College with a certificate in industrial technology. I worked last summer as an intern at Bio Products Corporation, and by the end of summer I was a member of a team that redesigned the computer training manual for Region Eight.

Confidence and Poise

Be enthusiastic and assertive and take an active role in the interview. For many people, interviewing is very frightening, and they react to their fear by acting passive. Passivity is a turnoff. You don't want to come across as arrogant, but acting submissive will lose you points. You are an equal human being. You want to be viewed as a professional and part of the team. Therefore, it is important to be confident and well prepared. Review the tips for overcoming shyness at the end of this chapter so that you will answer questions with confidence and ease.

If you focus on a positive attitude, you will be able to overcome your fear of interviewing. Focus your attention on the questions. Be ready for open-ended questions in which you can elaborate on the question asked. Most interviewers don't ask yes or no questions since they want you to talk and explain your background. Open-ended questions allow you to stress your skills and give specific examples of how you have demonstrated them. Be alert. Develop a winner's vocabulary that is positive and action-oriented. Relate your skills and assets to this position. Strong verbal skills help you create a confident image.

Verbal Skills

Words

Others form an impression of you by your choice of words. Assess the words you use to communicate.

Do you have a good vocabulary?

Do you know the language or buzzwords of the job?

Do you make sexist or racial slurs?

Do you use slang or overused words?

Do you use irritating or filler words such as *like, you know, uh?*

Do you use loaded words such as *honey* or *dear?*

Do you use formal names and titles when you first meet others?

Do you check for feedback from others that indicates understanding?

Do you have facts and figures to back up your material?

Can you make small talk?

Do you interrupt others?

Do you use direct and assertive words, or do you use qualifiers such as *kind of* or *sort of?*

Are you brief and to the point, or do you ramble?

Do you use common, concise words, or do you try to impress others with fancy or overly technical jargon?

Voice

What does your voice sound like? What are the positive aspects of your voice? Ask a good friend to be honest with you and let you know if you have annoying phrases or mannerisms that detract from your effectiveness as a communicator. Listen to yourself for a few days and jot down phrases that you tend to repeat.

After you have assessed your voice, set up an action plan to rid yourself of annoying habits. Join Toastmasters (a public speaking organization), take a speech class, go to a speech therapist, or ask a friend to help you improve.

Tape yourself and then listen carefully. Analyze your voice.

Positive aspects of your voice:	yes	no
Calm	——	——
Pleasant	——	——
Energetic	——	——
Confident	——	——
Reassuring	——	——
Crisp pronunciation	——	——
Warm tones	——	——
Energy and variety	——	——
Other:_____		

Negative aspects of your voice:	yes	no
Shrill	——	——
Strident	——	——
Grating	——	——
Strained	——	——
Raspy	——	——
Too rapid	——	——
Harsh	——	——
Breathy	——	——
Nasal	——	——
Abrasive	——	——
Slurring of words	——	——
Other:_____		

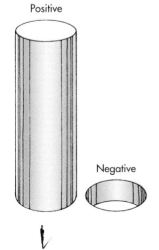

Positive

Negative

Positive Attitude

Your attitude at the beginning of an interview is the one factor that will most affect its outcome. Chapter 2 discussed the importance of motivation and a positive attitude for building contacts, staying enthusiastic, and making a good first impression. It is also critical to create a relaxed and positive mental state before and during the interview. If you have a negative outlook or go into an interview with a sense of doom, it will affect not only your thinking, but also your body language, dress, eye contact, tone of voice, and behavior. Anyone can internalize failure and dwell on faults, weaknesses, and shortcomings by maintaining, "I didn't have a chance in the interview anyway." Learn to relax by preparing, getting organized, rehearsing, and taking deep breaths.

Warmth and Humor

People who have a knack for building rapport are friendly and relaxed. They are able to laugh at themselves and life. Humor can put people at ease by bringing a light sense to even a tense situation. Humor, warmth, and a sincere smile create a comfortable climate. A nervous laugh, however, makes you look insecure and phony.

Respect and Etiquette

Your mother was right: Manners are important! Let's look at a few points of etiquette that are not only proper and nice, but essential for an effective interview.

Arrive on time and alone. If you're late for the interview, you've already said too much. Being late indicates you are inconsiderate, disorganized, or not serious about the job. If an emergency occurs, try to call and reschedule. Make certain you arrive at the building about 15–30 minutes before you are scheduled to be interviewed. Use that extra time to walk around, survey the area, read notes on bulletin boards, eat a light snack, get a cup of coffee, check yourself out in the mirror, and relax. Use the power of deep breathing to relax, project positive thoughts, and calmly review your notes about the company. Don't check in with the receptionist if you are more than 20 minutes early. Check in about 5 to 10 minutes before the interview. Chat with the receptionist; turn in an application (if you have not already submitted one). Be pleasant and positive.

Remember, get a good night's sleep and make certain that you get up early enough to have a healthy breakfast and avoid traffic problems and needless rushing about.

It is best to go on interviews alone. Unless the spouse is invited to a special event, bringing anyone with you for support is unprofessional. Also, it might indicate a lack of confidence that you certainly don't want to project.

Be respectful. While you understand your own nervousness, it is important to be sensitive to the interviewer and recognize that he or she may be a bit nervous, too. Good manners are always important, but never as much as in an interview. Civility means respect and sensitivity to the other person.

A Few Do's:

- Always be on time.
- Relax while sitting straight.
- Do everything you can to create a supportive climate. If you are offered coffee, have a cup. This creates a warm feeling of chatting with a friend or colleague and relaxes both of you.
- Follow your host in a subtle manner—if formal, be more formal; if relaxed, be more casual; and so on.
- Smile.
- Walk tall and use relaxed body language.
- Be confident. You are an equal professional.
- Make direct eye contact.
- Give a firm handshake.
- Take several deep breaths and focus on the positive.

A Few Don'ts:

- Don't chew gum or smoke.
- Don't drink alcohol or go to an interview with alcohol on your breath.
- Don't sit until the employer indicates the appropriate spot.
- Don't fidget or engage in nervous habits such as playing with your hair, keys, or coins.
- Don't look at your watch.
- Don't use first names unless you are invited to.
- Don't look fearful, anxious, overeager, arrogant, bored, or too passive.

Lunch and Dinner Interviews

Eating while you are being interviewed is especially difficult. Not only is the interviewer concerned with good answers, he or she is also concerned with your table manners, poise, confidence, and ability to make small talk. Your personality, demeanor, and attitude are the focus. Here are a few tips that can help:

1. Don't let down your guard. With light conversation, you might be tempted to slip into the role of being out for lunch with a friend, especially if you hit it off, discover you have several things in common, and share a few good laughs. But, remember, you are always being interviewed. *Maintain a professional demeanor.* Avoid taking a firm stance on politics or religion. You are here to get a job, not make a new best friend or persuade someone to follow your beliefs. Answer all questions professionally and use discretion. Follow the lead of the interviewer. Don't answer questions that haven't been asked, go into great detail about your personal life, or say anything negative about your past jobs or the people with whom you have worked.

2. Concentrate on the interview, not the meal. Order something light and easy to eat. Don't worry if you don't get full; you can grab a regular meal later when you are not distracted. Don't order ribs, corn on the cob, or any food that is messy and that you have to pick up with your hands. Your main concern should be on making a good impression, not on eating. Picture a job candidate who orders pork chops and with great relish, picks them up to clean off the bones. The image of grease running down his chin will overshadow positive traits and a glowing resumé! Remember, your first priority is to land the job, not to have a gourmet experience.

3. Use your best table manners. Learn which silverware to use. Put your napkin on your lap. Don't start eating until others have been served. Say please and thank you. Put your knife and fork on the side of your plate when you have finished and fold your napkin. Don't talk with your mouth full. Chew with your mouth closed. Yes, these are all things our mothers nagged us about, and they are critical in a job interview. Companies are concerned that employees make a good impression and know how to use good manners. This is especially important if you are dealing with the public or working with foreign markets, or if the company has an image that demands proper etiquette from all of its employers. **(continued)**

4. When ordering, take your lead from the interviewer. Ask what is recommended or the specialty of the restaurant. If in doubt, order something medium priced. Don't go for the most expensive or the least expensive item on the menu. Don't order toast if your interviewer is having a full meal.

5. Don't reach for the check. Even if the interviewer leaves it there for what may seem like a long time, you should not pick up the check. Remember, you are a guest.

6. Don't drink or smoke. Don't smoke even if you are invited to do so. Smoking will not enhance the interview. (However, if you are a non-smoker, don't make a fuss if the interviewer smokes.) Alcohol and nicotine are depressants and may cause you to appear jittery, nervous, and off guard. Some interviewers want to see how you handle alcohol. They also might want you to relax and be less inhibited so that you will offhandedly respond to revealing questions. In this relaxed setting, you may think this isn't really an interview. Don't blow it by thinking you can let your guard down after a few drinks.

Listening Skills

A large part of building rapport involves listening, not talking. Effective listening can make a difference in success or failure, not only in the job process, but in your career as well. Listen to the questions carefully. Pause before you jump in with your response. Don't interrupt the interviewer or change the subject. Show that you are interested by using good eye contact, nodding, smiling, and giving other reassurances that you understand. Active listening means listening to the intent of the speaker, not to just the words or tone.

Mirroring

One method of building rapport is to use the subtle technique of mirroring. You are not copying the interviewer's actions in a phony manner, but building a common bond through respect. Match your rate of speech, your posture, eye contact, phrases, and style to that of the interviewer. Stand in front of the couch or the chair to the left of the interviewer until you are asked to be seated. Your power position (if you are right-handed) is to have the interviewer sit on your right. Cross your legs to face the interviewer and lean slightly forward. You are creating a position that says, "See, we really are alike." People generally like others who are similar. It is always better to sit next to the interviewer rather than to sit with a desk between you. The desk creates a barrier that focuses on the roles you are each playing.

Compliment the interviewer on some positive aspect of the company that you discovered in your research, on something in the office, or a publication. Build rapport by focusing on similarities. What do you have in common?

In Chapter 3, we discussed how people learn, think, and relate using different styles. You can often tell a person's style by his or her nonverbal behavior, choice of words, and overall appearance. Listen carefully to how questions are framed.

If the interviewer appears to be a primarily a **thinker**, make certain you are accurate, more formal, and thoughtful in your responses and stress facts and detail. The overall message you want to create is "I do it right." The interviewer may use such phrases as, "Do you think . . ."

If the interviewer is primarily a **creator**, be idea oriented, flexible, friendly, and warm. The overall message you want to create is, "I am innovative, flexible, and creative." The interviewer may use such phrases as, "Do you see . . ."

If the interviewer is primarily a **relator**, be supportive and approachable, and stress harmony and cooperativeness. The overall message you want to create is, "I am compassionate, supportive, and a team player." The interviewer may use such phrases as, "How do you feel . . ."

If the interviewer is primarily a **director**, be results-oriented, logical, and stick to the subject. The overall message you want to create is, "I get results and am action-oriented." The interviewer may use such phrases as, "What have you accomplished . . ."

Step 6. Review Basic Questions and Answers

The interviewer will ask basic questions, and in answering you will be expected to restate qualifications and expand in certain areas. The purpose of this stage is to see how well you can communicate your skills, personality, and qualifications. If you have prepared for questions and practiced answering them, you will do well during this stage. Refer to Chapter 5 to refresh your memory about the most commonly asked questions and good responses. The main point is to relax and focus on the questions with the intention of answering them in a direct and honest manner.

The question behind the interviewer's question is Can you communicate in a direct and thoughtful manner? Your challenge is to have confident and thoughtful answers to basic questions and to clarify your skills and experiences. You must demonstrate that you have the necessary communication skills to speak in a clear, direct, and concise manner.

Step 7. Reinforce Your Skills and Strengths

At one stage in the interview, the questions will become more intense and probing. Remember, the resumé has already screened out people who are not qualified for the position. The basic question and answer session has clarified your skills. The interviewer now wants to know if you are the best person for the job. The purpose of this stage of the interview is to determine what specific skills and personal qualities you can bring to the company that would match their needs.

The question behind the interviewer's question is Why should we hire you? Your challenge is to demonstrate that you are the best applicant for the job.

The Competitive Edge: Focus on Personal Qualities

As has been stressed throughout this book, most companies look beyond job skills. That something extra is character and personality traits considered important for job success. Remember, the resumé and cover letter are used to screen out unqualified candidates. The interview is designed to find out what kind of person you are. The interviewer is attempting to assess your attitude, character, potential for growth, poise, communication skills, maturity, energy, temperament, and ability to solve problems. The underlying question is, Is this a good match? You must communicate that you have something unique to offer, that you can satisfy their needs, and that you really are the best person for this job.

In order to sell anything, it is important to know what the buyer wants. Most companies want to know the same things:

- Will this person fit in?
- Can this person solve problems?
- Can this person make sound decisions?
- Does this person have a positive attitude and enthusiasm?
- Can this person increase profits or decrease spending?

Here are a few general traits that most employers value in employees. How would you describe yourself and your work experiences to an interviewer to highlight and focus on these and other important traits?

- **Dependability.** You have the ability to keep agreements and follow through on commitments. You are on time.
- **Determination.** You have the desire and commitment to see a situation or goal through to completion even when problems or difficulties arise. You are persistent and get results.
- **Motivation.** You are enthusiastic and have the desire to achieve and be resourceful.
- **Honesty.** You have a strong moral sense of what is right. You are trustworthy
- **Integrity.** You take responsibility for your actions and hold your ground.
- **Empathy.** You have the ability to understand, actively listen and build rapport with others.
- **Cooperative.** You get along, are friendly, and work well with others.
- **Energetic.** You have the health and stamina to give time and effort to follow through on projects.

- **Confident.** You are poised, friendly, and self-assured, but not self-important or arrogant.
- **Persuasive.** You have the ability to speak and write in a clear, concise, effective and influential manner.
- **Organized.** You are efficient and effective and use the resources available to plan and achieve results.
- **Hardworking.** You are willing to go the extra mile, have demonstrated an industrious nature, and work in a consistent and sustained manner.
- **Initiative.** You have the ability to take initiative, to see what needs to be done, and to take action.
- **Flexible.** You are adaptable and can change directions at a moment's notice when necessary. You are prepared to pitch in and help out on different assignments.

EXERCISE 6.2 Make the Connection

Using the list of personality traits above, can you connect these traits to your experiences, background, and skills? What examples can you give? How can you highlight desirable personality traits and attributes?

1. The personal attribute I most want to highlight is:

   _____

2. I have demonstrated this attribute in the following ways:

   _____

3. Because of this quality, my work was affected in the following manner:

   _____

The following is an example demonstrating initiative:

> I helped my auto shop instructor grade papers and worked with him in the shop during labs. One time he didn't show up for class. I knew his wife was overdue on her delivery date for their first child. This was a night class and no administrators were on campus. I felt comfortable meeting the class. I gave the class several sample problems and broke them into groups. I also gave them a demonstration on motor repair since that is my area of specialty. My instructor was very appreciative that I took the initiative to go ahead with the class. The students said they enjoyed the demonstration and were kept on target with the class schedule.
>
> Because of this experience, I am more confident. I am careful not to overstep my bounds of authority, but I also know that there are times when it is important to take the initiative and get the job done.

Make a list of the personal qualities, skills, and abilities that you most want to get across in the interview. Next to each quality, write the experience that demonstrates this quality or skill. Review the self-assessment exercises in Chapter 1 and the work you did in Chapter 3 in translating your experiences into job skills. Make certain that your experience is true and that it demonstrates a positive quality. For example:

Quality	Demonstrates
Hardworking	I grew up on a farm, and I worked very hard before and after school, on weekends, and during summers.
Dependable	I have a part-time job and have never been late or missed a day of work.
Able to deal with stress	When my Dad lost his job, we had to really pull together. At the same time, my Grandmother was very ill. Everyone was under a lot of stress. I dealt with it by chipping in. I got a part-time job and helped take care of my Grandma. I learned a lot about budgeting my time, getting my priorities and values straight, and being a supportive part of a team.

The purpose of this exercise is to focus on the personal qualities and skills that you most want to get across during the interview. It condenses a mass of paperwork and a head full of ideas into the heart of who you are. Remember, these personal qualities and skills do not have to be work related. You can show how a life experience, a sport, a club event, travel, or a volunteer job helped you develop character, determination, skills, and so on.

Quality	Demonstrates
_____	_____
_____	_____
_____	_____
_____	_____
_____	_____
_____	_____
_____	_____
_____	_____

THE BENEFIT FACTOR:
Make Everything Count

The Benefit Factor

Determine the ways you can relate your accomplishments to specific situations. Relate school or college to your job. Discuss the jobs you held to work your way through college; special courses you took; and how you managed to juggle work, school, and activities. You might describe how you attended every class, played tapes while commuting, studied during small breaks throughout the day, and tackled difficult courses first. Writing reports and papers, giving speeches, making presentations, and compiling case studies are all important responsibilities of most jobs. A person who has done these tasks well in school can be a real asset to any company. Internships, part-time jobs, volunteer work in organizations, and community service should be highlighted as well since these activities can be directly translated into job skills.

Write a script about how you can describe each skill and the benefit that resulted from learning this skill:

Experience: On school newspaper staff for two years.

Skills learned and demonstrated: Learned writing and marketing skills. Learned to meet deadlines.

Cost benefit and benefit to company: Increased ads in school newspaper by 26 percent.

Action words to demonstrate benefit: marketing, cash management, innovation, quality enhancement, cost-reduction program, implementation, competitive analysis, marketplace penetration.

Other examples of accomplishments might include:

- Group problem-solving experiences.
- Helping to save a department from major cuts.
- Saving the company money.
- Cost-cutting measures you initiated.
- Tough deadlines that you met.
- Extra effort of working as a team.
- Training someone in new methods or new responsibilities.
- Increasing profits.
- Instituting a new system in manufacturing, marketing, accounting, and so on.
- Increasing sales by a certain percentage.
- Developing a new product or program.
- Developing new clients or affiliations or generating new business.
- Ability to work with diverse groups of people.

Step 8. Respond With Questions

The interviewer wants to see if the applicant can ask intelligent questions. The purpose of this stage is to give you a chance to assess how well you have done, to clarify certain points, clear up any miscommunications, and make certain you understand the job.

The question is can you leave a lasting positive impression by asking good questions? Your challenge is to ask thoughtful, intelligent, and probing questions.

Questions to Ask

Interviews are not one-sided. You are also probing for information and determining if a job is right for you and your career. Asking good questions also indicates to the interviewer that you have done your homework and that you are concerned about your career. Here are a few questions to help you size up whether this job is a window of opportunity or a closed door.

Be prepared to ask questions about the company, who you would be reporting to, the commitment to training and education, how important this position is to the company's mission, and so forth. During the interview, other questions may occur to you. Add them to a list of written questions. Don't try to memorize the questions you want to ask.

1. How does my position fit with the mission of the organization? What are the key responsibilities of this job?

2. What are the major challenges or concerns that face this organization in the near future?

3. Is the company planning major changes in the future? If so, how would they affect my department? My position?

4. Whom would I be working with most closely? Does this company use working teams?

5. Ideally, what would you like me to contribute to this organization? What skills and personality characteristics are most important for success at this company?

6. How would you describe the corporate culture at this organization? The management style?

7. Who are your major competitors?

8. What is the major difference between this company and your competitors?

9. What do you wish you had known about this company when you interviewed for your position? What is it about the company that attracted you or has caused you to stay?

10. How do you view company morale? What is the company's philosophy about motivating employees?

11. Besides making a profit and offering good service, what values are most important at this company?

12. I have read your mission statement. How do you make this philosophy come alive on a daily basis for your employees and customers?

13. I plan on working hard and contributing to the company. What advancement do you see for me in five years if I have proven myself?

14. What are the major goals of this company in the near future?

15. How many people have held this job in the last 10 years? Where did they go?

Of course, you will want to see a written job description; understand your key assignments, whom you will be reporting to, who reports to you, what the travel requirements are, and what the company's performance review procedure is; and find out where your office will be.

Questions Not to Ask

Do not bring up salary, vacations, benefits, or sick leave until the interviewer brings them up or until you are offered the position. You should, however, have in mind a realistic salary that is acceptable to you. Find out what the going rate is for similar jobs at various companies. Differentiate between what you desire and what you will accept. If you are asked what you expect, you can respond with a range.

Questions a Job Interviewer Should Not Ask You

You may be asked questions that are inappropriate and in some cases, illegal, as prohibited by *The Americans with Disabilities Act of 1990.** How you answer such questions—your body language and demeanor—is just as important as the words you use. Answering such questions in a tactful way will be a challenge.

It is best not to become defensive or angry. Most interviewers are attempting to gather information about you in such subtle areas as personality, attitudes, and general ability to learn and change. Look beyond the question and attempt to determine what it is the interviewer is trying to get you to reveal. Remember, the employer is trying to find a "fit"—someone who will be an integral part of the team. Given that most employers have honorable intentions, get beyond the question to what they really want to know.

Laws change, but the following are some sensitive areas that are taboo or at the very least inappropriate:

Age: Federal law protects against age discrimination. *How old are you? How old are your children?* or other questions that attempt to determine age are inappropriate and taboo. Special laws, however, do exist for the employment of minors and for people over 70. If you are young, the employer may want to determine if you are mature and have the necessary experience and wisdom to make sound decisions. If you are an older applicant, the employer may want to determine if you are set in your ways, if you have enough energy to do the job, if you have health problems associated with growing older, if you can relate to younger staff and customers, and so on.

Marital status: The general rule is that a woman should not be asked any question that wouldn't also be asked of a man and that all questions should be job related. Questions about children, child care, spouse's employment, and birth control are illegal. If an interviewer is concerned whether a married candidate would be able to travel extensively, it is appropriate to ask: *Will extensive traveling be a problem for you?* but not, *Does your husband mind if you travel?* The employer may also want someone who is dependable, can give a lot of time and energy to the job, and who is willing to relocate.

*For more information on illegal questions, see *The Americans with Disabilities Act* by Joan Ackerstein, J. D., (Burr Ridge, IL: Richard D. Irwin, Inc.).

Sexual preference: It is taboo to question someone's sexual preference: *Would your lifestyle be an embarrassment to this company?* The employer may be concerned about how discreet you are about your private life and if you will offend other staff or customers.

Religion: You should never be asked about your religion (unless you are applying to a religious organization). However, if an interviewer is concerned, for example, about whether you will be able to work at certain times, it is appropriate to ask, *Can you work occasionally on Saturday, Sunday, or certain holidays?*

Race or national origin: You should not be asked what your race or nationality is. Nor should you be asked for a picture of yourself.

Handicaps: You should not be asked questions about a physical or mental handicap unless it will directly affect job performance. You can be asked such questions as, This position requires long hours sitting at the computer. *Do you have any physical problems that would directly affect your job performance?*

Financial matters: Questions about your financial affairs—such as *Do you own your own home?*—are taboo. However, in many states, employers are allowed to run standard credit checks on potential candidates. Employers may be trying to find out how stable an applicant is.

Criminal record: You should not be asked, Have you ever been arrested? However, it is not illegal to ask if you have ever been convicted of a crime. Employers value honesty and want to feel assured that they can trust employees.

How to Respond

Hiring and training new people is expensive. Therefore, employers are concerned about getting the best possible candidate and finding out as much as possible about that person. You may get asked some questions that make you feel uncomfortable. If you want the job, the best advice is to remain calm and respond in such a way that lets the interviewer know you can read beyond the inappropriate question. Don't get defensive. Let's say you are asked how many children you have. You know that the interviewer wants to find out if you will be dependable. You might reply as follows:

> I have three children. I understand that this job would require me to work weekends and nights. That will not be a problem. I have excellent day care and several backup caretakers. I am committed to getting the job done and producing excellent results. That often means putting in additional hours. I am dependable and only missed two days of work last year as a result of illness at my last job.

Remember, this is not a battleground to prove who is right. You do not have to allow anyone to intimidate or embarrass you, but you can also learn to respond with tact and respect.

Since everyone has some characteristic or situation that may be perceived as a handicap, it is often better to bring it out in the open in a positive light and discuss how you would deal with it. For example, say you are 20 years old and just graduated from a certificate program in real estate. You can anticipate that the interviewer may have concerns and ask a question about your lack of experience and youth. Instead of hiding from this issue, why not face it and respond directly:

> I have a lot of energy and stamina. I am eager to learn, open to change, and have not formed negative habits. I am enthusiastic, hardworking, and am willing to work very hard to learn this business. I work well with people of all ages and do not mind taking orders or following directions.

Or, suppose you are a single woman who has sole custody of four small children. Rather than hide from the situation, bring up the issue of dependability and assure the interviewer that you are adequately prepared:

> I have a live-in housekeeper, backup day care, and family and friends who help in case of an emergency. In my last position, I only took off a few days because of family illness and even then I was able to complete work at home. I am dependable and committed to my profession.

Make certain you are prepared to discuss questions that assess your potential weaknesses. Review Exercise 5.2 and give careful consideration to good responses.

EXERCISE 6.4   Responding to Difficult Questions

Respond to the following questions. Make up other questions and responses that you think you may be asked.

1. Can you explain why your grades were not very good in school?

    _____

2. Your job experience is limited to the fast-food industry. Have you had any other experiences in which to demonstrate your skills?

    _____

3. Do you think your lack of a college degree will hinder your career goals?

    _____

4. _____

5. _____

6. _____

Step 9. Readjust, Correct, and Close

As you are interviewing, pay attention to eye contact and body language. You may notice when someone is giving you the signal to move on, or you may pick up clues that he or she is confused or disagrees with what you are saying. Of course, you don't want to waffle in your presentation, but you should be sensitive to body cues and feedback and adjust your answers accordingly. For example, If you are getting a puzzled look, ask the interviewer if examples or clarification would be helpful. The important thing to remember at this stage is to be sensitive, aware, fully in the present, and flexible. Successful people have the ability to adjust and adapt to different situations.

Generally when the interview is winding down, the interviewer will ask if you have any questions. In addition to asking questions, this is also the time to summarize your strengths and stress how they relate to the job. For example:

> Thank you for the opportunity to discuss how my strengths in organization and writing and my computer skills relate to this position. I know I could make a real contribution to your company. I am very excited about this position and how well it matches my strengths.

Here are a few other tips to follow for making the closing a success:

1. Etiquette and good manners. Many interviews require a great deal of time, cost, and coordination. Express your appreciation to your host. Make certain that you recognize the hospitality and professionalism of the staff. For example: Thank you for the opportunity to interview for this position. I very much appreciate your time and the professional way you handled the interview.

2. Follow up with interest. You may find yourself exhausted from the trip, questions, and tour, but keep up your energy and attention. Show your interest and enthusiasm for the job right through to the end of the interview. Take note of any new developments, equipment, or programs that are mentioned or noticed during a tour or discussion and refer to them at the end of the interview.

3. Follow up with questions. You will usually be asked if you have any final questions, so have a few ready. Ask specific questions about the company and the job when appropriate. Demonstrate that you have done your homework.

4. Follow up with details. Make certain you know what is expected next. Ask when you might expect to hear about the decision and who will call you. Check to make certain they have your phone number and where you can best be reached at that time. The interviewer will usually indicate an approximate date for notification. If not, ask when you might hear and if you could call in a week or so. Generally, you will not be offered the job on the spot. If you are, however, indicate that you would like a few days to think about it. Ask when they need an answer.

Reassessing the interview, follow-up, and negotiating salary will be covered in Chapter 7.

THE NOMADIC WORKFORCE

Workplace Trends

Key: Mobility and Autonomy

Many organizations have taken their offices on the road. An increasing number of employees are booting up their laptop computers in hotel rooms and at customer sites, and setting up makeshift offices wherever it makes most sense. For many companies, this means their employees are building relationships with customers rather than sitting in meetings at the corporate headquarters. Many workers in sales and management spend 80 percent of their time on the road, only coming into the main office to meet with co-workers. They access their messages from voice mail and their appointments from E-mail and send messages across the country as though they were in the office next door. Employees travel with their computers, financial records, calendars, and proposals.

The advantage of the virtual or temporary workplace is lower cost—expensive office space can be reduced or eliminated, and instant decisions can be made. A by-product of the computer age is the accessibility of information. Information is shared among all staff instantly and no longer hoarded by top executives. In the past decisions were delayed until management was back in the office. Now decisions can be made anywhere, at any time. This new breed of nomadic workers is changing the face of the workplace and putting more emphasis on production, customer service, and instant response.

Career Strategies: Be a flexible self-starter and develop good work habits.

HITTING THE WALL

Scaling the Wall

Most people experience anxiety and apprehension when they interview for a job. But for the shy job hunter, interviewing can be truly painful. Making face-to-face contact becomes a huge obstacle. You may experience self-doubt as you interview for jobs. Perhaps you had an interview where you did not anticipate certain questions, that caused you anxiety and left you flustered. You may even start to avoid applying for jobs you really want because you fear rejection. Don't let the fear of rejection dampen your confidence. Learn to overcome your shyness.

Scaling the Wall

Here are a few tips to help you overcome shyness:

1. Build a strong network. For a shy person, networking is vital. Networking can connect you to qualified, supportive, and competent people who can provide you with support, advice, courage, connections, and feedback.

2. Use the power of teamwork. Form a job-strategy team and get together with several other people who are also shy to discuss strategies and concerns. Offer each other support and encouragement. Practice interviewing and giving each other feedback. Continue meeting with your team even after you have found your job. Discuss promotions, networking on the job, performance reviews, and ways to increase your visibility. Join Toastmasters, a public speaking club, and learn to overcome stage fright and become a better speaker.

3. Learn to be an active listener. You can use your shyness to become an effective and active listener. During an interview, you can develop rapport by using good eye contact, showing interest, and giving thoughtful answers. You will be valued for your good listening skills, and you will find that shyness disappears when you focus on the other person.

4. Visualize yourself as confident. Use the power of the mind to vividly imagine yourself walking tall, smiling warmly, shaking hands, making direct eye contact, and giving great answers to difficult questions. See yourself poised, confident, and at ease. Consciously learn to reprogram your self-talk with positive affirmations instead of negative put-downs. Watch confident, self-assured people. How do they walk, talk, and gesture? Notice their eye contact, their listening skills, the questions they ask, and so on. Model the behaviors you want to learn.

5. Concentrate on the other person. Shy people often worry about how other people are seeing them and fret over events that haven't even happened yet. Learn to live fully in the moment. Concentrate on the interview questions and building rapport with the interviewer. Say to yourself, How can I make this person feel comfortable?

The Knockout Factor

- Poor personal appearance.
- Poor communication skills, little eye contact, nervousness.
- Lack of enthusiasm, interest, and vitality, or a negative attitude.
- Lack of confidence or poise.
- Lack of maturity. No career goals or sense of direction.
- Overbearing or aggressive "know-it-all" attitude.
- Lack of knowledge of company or field.
- Lack of respect or etiquette.
- Failure to demonstrate skills or how strengths relate to job.
- Failure to respond with good questions.

The Success Factor

- Professional and appropriate appearance.
- Good verbal and nonverbal communication skills.
- Positive attitude and enthusiasm.
- Confident, poised, and friendly.
- Mature, well-thought-out career goals.
- A sense of humility and grace.
- Well prepared and knowledgeable.
- Respectful, well mannered, a good listener.
- Ability to communicate how skills and strengths would benefit the company.
- Good questions.
- Ability to speak in a clear, concise, correct, and direct manner.

PROBLEM SOLVING AT WORK

Problem Solving

Jerry is 20 and has just graduated from a college with an associate's degree in heating, air-conditioning, and technology. He is eager to start working full-time and wants to work at the same company where he has worked part-time while attending school. He has put together a resumé and a good cover letter, and has prepared good questions and answers. Jerry is well prepared for the interview. However, he is very shy and has always avoided any kind of public speaking. He is terrified of the interview and breaks out in a sweat just thinking about it. Here is how Jerry used creative problem-solving to explore solutions and critical thinking to make his decision.

1. Have I clearly stated the problems? How can I overcome my fear of speaking and interviewing?

> **Define problem:** I want to create a positive first impression and have a successful interview. How can I overcome my fear, build rapport, and create a positive first impression?
>
> **What:** What questions will be asked of me? What questions should I ask? What can I do that will meet my objective of overcoming my shyness?
>
> **Who:** Who will be interviewing me, and how can I build rapport? Who should I contact to overcome my shyness?
>
> **When:** When is the interview? When should I invest the time and energy to overcome my stage fright?
>
> **Where:** Where is the interview? Where do I go to get help in overcoming my shyness?
>
> **How:** How can I create a professional image and build rapport? How can I make the connection between my skills, abilities, and accomplishments and the needs of the employer? How can I transform my shyness and learn better speaking and presentation skills?

2. Do I have enough information? Do I have all the information I need to make a decision? Have I researched the benefits of public speaking, and have I controlled my fears? Have I prepared for the interview?

3. Can I make the decision by myself? What resources are available to help me make a better decision? Have I talked with a career counselor, my advisor, my instructors?

4. Have I brainstormed alternatives? What other methods are available? Could I start by talking with someone from Toastmasters or a speech teacher?

5. Have I looked at likely consequences? If I begin to overcome my fear of speaking and interviewing will I increase my chances of getting a job? What other consequences might occur if I don't overcome my fears?

6. Have I identified all the resources and tools needed? Have I researched the resources available? Am I aware of Toastmasters and speech classes to overcome my shyness and help me develop better communication skills? Am I willing to acquire the additional skills and tools to be successful?

7. Have I developed and implemented an action plan?

Have I designed an action plan that will help me make sound decisions or am I doing what feels safe and comfortable?

8. Have I identified the best solution and done everything possible to ensure success?

Have I made a decision using critical thinking and creativity? Am I committed to making the decision a success? Have I written down all the details concerning the interview?

9. Have I assessed the results?

Have I evaluated my decision to see if it is working? Have I assessed my progress?

10. Have I modified the plan, if necessary?

What adjustments could I make that would make my decision more successful?

Interviewing Strategies

- Relax and overcome fear, anxiety, and shyness.
- Project a confident and professional image.
- Be enthusiastic and project a positive attitude.
- Be respectful and use good business etiquette.
- Build rapport. Be a good listener.
- Be in the present and respond with good answers.
- Demonstrate how you will benefit the company.
- Readjust and correct your presentation.
- Ask good questions.
- Close, review, and assess.

Chapter Checklist   Yes   No

1. **Have you learned how to relax?**
   Overcome fear and shyness?

2. **Do you know how to create a positive first impression?**
   Nonverbal communication
   Direct eye contact.
   Pleasing smile.
   Firm handshake.
   Good posture.
   Poised.

   Verbal communication
   Grammar.
   Vocabulary.
   Pleasing voice.
   Clear and concise.
   Self-expression.

3. **Do you know how to answer basic questions with**
   Good answers?
   Clear, concise communication skills?
   Good speaking voice?
   Credible style?
   Good vocabulary?
   Correct grammar?

4. **Do you know how to reinforce skills and achievements? Can you**
   Clearly communicate skills?
   Sell yourself as the person the employer should hire?
   Connect achievements with needs of the company?
   Give examples of skills and experience?

5. **Can you effectively respond with questions?**
   Questions are well thought out.
   Good common sense.
   Tactful.
   Relate job qualifications to skills.

6. **Can you readjust and close?**
   Readjust questions.
   Stress abilities and achievements.
   Close the interview.

Follow-Up Strategies That Work

Introduction

After the interview, you may be tempted to breathe a sigh of relief and believe the only thing you have left to do is wait. However tempting it is to take a break, it is crucial that you stay active, involved, and focused. Waiting will not get you the job. This chapter will look at the importance of following up on the seemingly small details that can make the difference in a successful job search.

—

Learning Objectives

In Chapter 7, you will learn

- The importance of follow-up letters, calls, and contacts.

- How to reassess and evaluate the interview process.

- How to write thank-you notes.

- How to clarify expectations and agreements.

- Effective negotiation strategies.

Why Is Follow-Up So Important?

Following up on details is an essential part of the job search. In fact, following up on the interview is almost as important as the interview itself. Without follow-up, your cover letter and resumé may end up lost, set aside, buried on someone's desk, or forgotten. You may have had a great interview, but as weeks pass, the interviewer may forget which candidate said what or how impressive your skills really are. A thank-you note will help the interviewer remember your strengths and achievements or take a second look at your resumé. In addition to writing thank-you notes, follow-up means assessing your interview performance and progress, writing letters in response to rejections, following up with phone calls, sending out more resumés—in short, staying active in the job search until you get and accept an offer. As the old saying goes,"It's not over until it's over." Even when you have a solid offer, follow-up is important. Negotiating the best salary, making a sound decision about whether or not to accept the offer, and keeping good records are all follow-up tasks that are important for your career.

Reassessment

As soon as possible after the interview, find a quiet spot and jot down your immediate thoughts concerning the interview. Make certain you have the correct names and spelling of everyone who interviewed you or key people to whom you were introduced. If you need to send in additional material or were given a date when a decision will be made, jot this down.

When you have more time, sit back and, in a nonjudgmental and detached way, review and reassess the interview. What did you feel comfortable about? What questions were a surprise? Did you feel you had rapport? What would you do differently if you could? The point of this reviewing is not to worry or fret, but to improve. Use a checklist like the one in Exercise 7.1, to review each aspect of the interview.

Date   Company

_____   _____

Job Position   Interviewer's name

_____   _____

Questions	**Yes**	**No**
1. I researched the company.	___	___
2. I researched the industry.	___	___
3. I focused on the employer's needs.	___	___
4. I made a positive first impression.	___	___
5. My greeting was professional and friendly.	___	___
6. I communicated my achievements in a direct and concise manner.	___	___
7. I listened carefully and responded sincerely.	___	___
8. I adjusted my verbal and nonverbal communication when needed.	___	___
9. I emphasized personal qualities.	___	___
10. I successfully channeled excess energy and was relaxed and calm.	___	___
11. I related personal traits and strengths to the position.	___	___
12. I showed courtesy, respect, and good manners.	___	___
13. I expressed focused and mature career goals.	___	___
14. I showed energy and enthusiasm.		
15. I successfully adapted to the style of the interviewer.	___	___
16. I successfully answered difficult questions with poise.	___	___
17. I clarified the decision-making process.	___	___
18. I asked good questions and gathered valuable information.	___	___
19. My closing was strong and focused.	___	___

My overall feeling about the interview:

_____

Which questions did I feel most comfortable with?

_____

Which questions did I feel least comfortable with?

_____

If I had the interview to do over again, what would I do differently?

_____

Follow Up with a Thank-You Note

After you have finished your initial assessment of the interview, take time to write a thank-you note. A thank-you note not only communicates good business etiquette, it communicates your attention to detail and ability to build rapport. Express your favorable impression of the company, your appreciation for the interview, and your continued interest in the position. You can cite specific examples.

Because few people take the time to write them, a thank-you note is a great way to set yourself apart from others who have interviewed for the same position. It is also a written reminder of who you are and will solidify your image in the mind of the interviewer.

Send a thank-you note, not only to the interviewer, but to anyone who you enjoyed talking to or who was especially helpful, such as the receptionist, department head, professionals in your field, someone in your network, or potential co-workers who took time to meet with you. These people may be able to give you a recommendation, leads on another job, or keep you in mind for the future.

Your thank-you note can be either handwritten or typed. The following are guidelines for all thank-you notes:

- Send a thank-you note within 24 hours.
- Make certain spelling and grammar are correct.
- Check the proper spelling of people's names and titles.
- Keep notes short and concise, but sincere.
- Mention your interest in working with the company.
- Thank anyone who has been helpful.
- Make notes personal and individual.

Example of a sample handwritten thank-you note

January 18, 1995

Dear Ms. Wilson,

Thank you for the time you spent with me on Thursday. You conducted a very professional and informative interview. I am now even more interested in working for Colony Electronic Company.

I am impressed with the department's high standards of quality and your personal commitment to customer satisfaction.

I am most interested in being part of the marketing team. I believe that my strong public relations background could help Colony become even more successful.

Sincerely,

Jan Baily

Use the standard format for a business letter (the same format you followed when writing cover letters), for a formal typed thank-you note.

Note: With computers or a word processor, it is easy to create a letterhead with your return address or you can put your address under your name as in the following sample.

April 28, 199_   *Date*
                                           (1–2 inches from top of paper)

Ms. Loretta Finch
Director, Human Relations Department
Capital Industry
2202 Bend Street
Pinecrest, Alabama 23993

                                       Inside address
                                       (4–6 spaces)
Dear Ms. Finch: *Salutation*
                                       (2–3 spaces)

Thank you for an enjoyable interview last Friday. The interview was conducted professionally, and everyone I met was helpful and pleasant. I enjoyed learning more about Capital Industry and have a sincere desire to work for this progressive and supportive company. I was most impressed with your training program.

                                   Body (2 spaces)
If additional information is needed, please let me know. I look forward to hearing from you.

Sincerely,   *Complimentary Close*
                                     (3–4 spaces)

John L. McAllen   *Signature*

John L. McAllen
2910 Greenbriar Lane   *Return address*
Troy, Michigan 48002

Enclosures   *Additional information*

Write a sample thank-you note for a recent interview or use the following example:

Interviewer's name:	Ms. Jan Ross
Title:	Director of Human Resources
Company:	Research Biological
Job position:	Research technician

Follow Up Systematically—Stay Organized

You can decrease the frustration on your job search and increase its effectiveness if you continue to use the systematic record-keeping system discussed in Chapter 2. Don't rely on your memory or feel that once you have gone through this process, you can forget the required steps. Most people change jobs several times in their career. If you set up an effective record-keeping system, you will be able to review the process easily, minimizing frustrations and enhancing your confidence and job-search skills. Keeping meticulous records will also help you be successful in your job and get promoted. For example, keep records of your goals, achievements, successful projects, letters of appreciation, and so forth. These will be important during performance reviews and for your own goal setting.

Keep Networking

Let your references and the key people who helped you in your job search know if you have interviewed for a job and how your job search is going. They may be able to give you information about other jobs.

Networking isn't just a job-search activity, it's a vital part of career success. Review your network often and follow up with information concerning your job search and your career. Set goals for meeting new people and nurturing long-term professional contacts. Be supportive of co-workers, professional contacts, and friends. Send thank-you notes, articles of interest, notes of concern, and congratulations for achievements to your network when appropriate. Listen actively and be there when people need support.

Keep a Job Search Journal

It is difficult to remember what you have accomplished and the progress you're making in your job search. Jot down details, names, dates, important information, and your emotional highs and lows as they occur. A journal can be extremely valuable throughout your job search and in your career.

Keep Up with Telephone Callbacks

It is critical to keep a complete list of those companies you have sent resumés and where you've interviewed. In your cover letter and during an interview, you will have indicated that you will call them at a certain time to schedule a time to meet. Make your calls promptly as a reminder that you sent your resumé, are interested in the position, and would very much like an interview. (Or in the case of a post-interview call, that you are calling to follow up the interview itself). If you call and cannot reach the person who has the power to hire, follow up with another letter indicating your interest and a time when you will call again. Sometimes it takes several phone calls before you are able to speak directly to the person who has the authority or information you want.

Stay in continual contact with prospective employers. Polite persistence is a major factor in getting a job.

Other Follow-Up Letters

It is not enough just to send your cover letter and resumé. It is important to follow up in a week or so for a reminder and to keep your name in recognition. Send another resumé with this follow-up letter such as the one on the next page.

Example of a first follow-up letter requesting an interview

July 7, 199_

Ms. Loretta Finch
Director, Human Relations Department
Capital Industry
2202 Bend Street
Pinecrest, Alabama 23993

Dear Ms. Finch:

On June 30, I applied to Capital Industry for a position as sales representative in the Midwest region. As I haven't heard from you, I wanted to let you know I am still very interested in working for your company.

Over the last few months, I have done considerable research into Capital Industry. I am impressed with the progressive marketing and quality of products. Customer service is stressed and your distributor in Austin expressed support for your training and service.

As my resumé indicates, I have demonstrated the following:

• A positive attitude and outgoing personality.
• Effective communication skills and success in working as a team.
• Self-motivation and a willingness to learn by continually taking courses and workshops since earning an associates degree in business.
• Capacity for hard work, dependability, and responsibility.

I am confident I can make a real contribution to Capital Industry. I would appreciate the opportunity to meet with you and discuss these ideas. I will call next week to see if we can arrange a mutually convenient time.
Thank you for your consideration.

Sincerely,

John L. M°Allen

John L. McAllen
2910 Greenbriar Lane
Troy, Michigan 48002

YOU GOT THE JOB!

You will usually receive a call from the interviewer offering you the job. At this time, you may be offered a specific salary, or the interviewer may ask you to come in to discuss salary and benefit details. This phone call or negotiation meeting is generally followed by a formal letter outlining the salary agreement, the starting date of the job, and where to report the first day. Before you accept a salary, spend some time thinking about how you will negotiate it.

Follow Up with Negotiations

Congratulations! You have been offered the job! Now the time has come to negotiate your salary. The question to ask yourself is, "How much am I worth?" Your answer will likely affect the outcome of your salary negotiation. You must convince both yourself and the employer of the value you bring to the job.

Researching the market value of your field, your employer, your position, and your skills is crucial. Come up with a range of high and low salaries that employees in similar positions are earning. Several resources will be useful in identifying current salaries: professional trade organizations, business magazines, company literature, and contacts in the field. Check with your local library for additional resources. Keep a file of salary ranges and job descriptions of areas you are interested in. This file should be kept and updated throughout your career.

Always keep in mind that salaries will vary by geographical locations. So check out the cost of living for the area where you wish to work to make comparisons. Government offices also have standardized salary schedules, which are published by the Department of Labor.

During negotiation you may be asked to tell the employer what salary you have in mind. Avoid presenting your requirements first. Respond by saying that you need to know more about the job assignment, advancement possibilities, and training. Ask the employer to provide you with a range for entry-level jobs at the company and compare the range with your research. Discuss your worth and the value you will add to the organization. Your experience, skills, personal qualities, and education are valuable.

Be careful not to paint yourself into a corner. If you state a salary that is too low, the employer may question your worth and self-confidence. You may also be resentful later if you settle for less money than other people are making with your experience and background.

If you state a salary that is too high, however, it may disqualify you. If you already have a job, you will generally want to increase your salary.

You might say, "I would expect to make what other customer service reps make with my training and experience and am certain that your offer would come into that range. I am most concerned about a good commission plan and that my salary will reflect my ability to produce results." If you are offered the lowest salary and you think your training and experience are worth more, counter with a somewhat higher salary that still keeps you within the range. Show that you have self-worth and negotiation skills.

Beyond Salary

Take a moment to go over all details and make certain you and your new supervisor agree on them. Ask for a job description. The time to clarify expectations is before you sign the acceptance letter.

Factors	Agreement
Salary.	
Benefits.	
Vacation and holidays.	
Insurance.	
Retirement plan.	
Starting date.	
Office space.	
Specific responsibilities and expectations.	
Supervisor.	
Nature of performance reviews.	
Raises and promotion.	
Daily schedule and overtime or normal work expectations.	
Travel.	
Procedures for travel reimbursements.	
Relocation.	

EXERCISE 7.3   Evaluate Your Decision

Ask yourself several questions about any company before you make a final commitment:

- Is it economically stable?
- Is it the right size and in the right location for my style and needs?
- Are the pay and benefits adequate?
- Is the company technologically current?
- Is there emphasis on research and development of new products?
- Is there a good training program?
- Can I work toward my long-term career goals at this company?
- Is family and leisure time important to the company?
- How much travel is expected?
- Is there a strong commitment to corporate ethics?

Write an Acceptance Letter

Once you feel you have made a rational and sound decision, it's time to write an acceptance letter. An acceptance letter provides a formal written record of your acceptance for both you and the interviewer. This is your opportunity to:

1. Indicate enthusiasm.
2. Express appreciation.
3. Clarify and agree to the conditions of your employment.
4. Provide an address and phone number where you can be reached.

Sample acceptance letter

John L. McAllen
2910 Greenbriar Lane, Troy, Michigan 48002

April 28, 1995

Ms. Loretta Finch
Director, Human Relations Department
Capital Industry
2202 Bend Street
Pinecrest, Alabama 23993

Dear Ms. Finch:

Thank you for your call Tuesday informing me that I have been chosen for the position of sales representative. I am eager to become part of the team at Capital Industry and am confident that I will contribute to the company.

I have appreciated your consideration during the interview process. The entire job process was made enjoyable because of your professional style.

I will arrive for work in three weeks (May 15). I can be reached at my parents' home until then. Their address and phone number are:

Jan and Bill McAllen
331 Greenbriar Lane
Pinecrest, Alabama 23993
(202)839-0032

Thanks again for your support. I look forward to working with you.

Sincerely,

John L. McAllen

John L. McAllen

When You Don't Get a Job Offer

Even if you don't do well in an interview or you hear that the job was offered to someone else, write thank-you notes to those companies that you still find interesting. You never know when another opening will occur. The interviewer will think of you and your well-written thank-you note, recognizing your grace and professionalism. This type of thank-you note should express appreciation for the interview, continued interest in the company, and best wishes for the company's success. The following letter is an example:

Sample rejection letter response

John L. McAllen
2910 Greenbriar Lane, Troy, Michigan 48002

April 28, 199_

Ms. Loretta Finch
Director, Human Relations Department
Capital Industry
2202 Bend Street
Pinecrest, Alabama 23993

Dear Ms. Finch:

Thank you for sending me the letter informing me that you have chosen another candidate for the position of sales representative for the Midwest division of Capital Industry.

I was treated with professional courtesy by everyone I met, and the entire review process was enjoyable. You have been most helpful and considerate.

I wish you the best with the new candidate. If another position does open up in the near future, please keep me in mind. I am still very interested in Capital Industry and believe I could make a real contribution.

Thank you again for your time and consideration.

Sincerely,

John L. M°Allen

John L. McAllen

EXERCISE 7.4 Assessment

Are you getting interviews? Have you been prepared for the interviews? Use the following guidelines to assess your job-search process. Consider incorporating this checklist into a daily log.

Date:

_____

I have done my homework and completed research for the following companies:

_____

I have sent out resumés, personalized cover letters, and prepared for interviews for the following companies:

_____

I have prepared for interviews and interviewed for the following positions:

_____

My feelings about today's interviews and calls are:

_____

Take Time to Reevaluate

Using the checklists at the end of each chapter, make certain you have followed the strategies of a successful job search. What is going right and wrong with your job search? Are you making progress? Start logging replies and your analysis of interviews, and begin the process of determining whether your plan of action is effective. Your goal is to get invited for an interview and get a job offer. If you are working hard at the job search but are becoming discouraged, this is the time to reevaluate your efforts. Find out what is keeping you from being successful. Were you late for an interview? Are there strategies you need to practice more? Review the exercises you've done throughout this book for help in assessing interests and skills, and writing and presentation skills.

Assess possible reasons why you are not getting job offers. You may not be realistic applying for certain jobs. Or you may be falling victim to one of the reasons below.

Most Common Reasons for Job Turndown

- Unprofessional appearance.
- Indifference and lack of enthusiasm.
- Excessive nervousness.
- Know-it-all attitude.
- Little eye contact and lack of poise and self-confidence.
- Lack of preparation. Did not do homework on company.
- Poor communication skills.
- Did not relate skills and strengths to job.
- Poor manners.
- Misrepresented qualifications.

But the good news is that all these reasons can be countered by following the strategies and guidelines presented in this book. Use the list below as a road map for reviewing the strategies you need to increase your chance of success.

Ten Strategies That Work

1. Improve your appearance (Chapter 5).
2. Positive, enthusiastic attitude (Chapters 5, 6, 7, and 8).
3. Relaxed manner (Chapter 6).
4. Ability to build rapport (Chapter 6).
5. Confident, and poised, direct eye contact (Chapters 5 and 6).
6. Well prepared (Chapters 1, 2, and 5).
7. Effective verbal and nonverbal communication skills (Chapters 5 and 6).
8. Ability to effectively relate skills and strengths to job (Chapters 1, 3, 4, 5, and 6).
9. Good manners and effective listener (Chapters 5 and 6).
10. Honesty and integrity (Chapters 3 and 5).

THE BENEFIT FACTOR

The Benefit Factor

Serving as a mentor can be one of the most rewarding aspects of your career, Having a mentor can greatly enhance your job search and career. Now that you have learned and applied many job-search strategies, you may want to help others benefit from your knowledge and experience. Consider serving as a mentor for a person who is just beginning the job-search process. You may want to call your school or college and volunteer to act as an alumni resource for other students who will be looking for jobs. Benefit others by helping them build their professional network.

Use all the resources you have developed during your job search to help you benefit your career. Continue to build your network and develop a mentor relationship. A mentor can give advice, coach, encourage, help you with career decisions, and provide visibility.

THE NEW WORK TEAMS

Key: Cooperative Team Player
The old image of the ambitious, young employee working independently as he or she is moving up the corporate ladder has been replaced by a large and intricate web of work teams. The corporate star who looks for the fast track to promotions will find that teamwork is often the most valuable skill to have. More and more companies are replacing management layers with independent work teams. Creative thinking, the ability to work with others, and innovative approaches to problems will be valued more than titles, seniority, age, and degrees. Instead of a supervisor, work teams will monitor and supervise each other. They will be formed to solve certain key problems and then be rearranged or disbanded. For example a work team packaging potato chips may be involved in processing, packaging, equipment maintenance, pricing, quality control, service performance, marketing, and customer satisfaction. Some work teams will be involved in every stage of production from start to finish, which benefits the company in terms of increased productivity, pride, and autonomy. Other work teams will be brought together to complete a special task or project or to troubleshoot and then be disbanded.

Working in integrated product-development teams, people have the opportunity to learn new skills and understand how other departments fit into production. For example, a diverse team may be involved in product design, marketing, and customer service. In order to be successful, team members must learn responsibility, problem solving, decision making, trust, team spirit, and quality control. The benefit to workers is empowerment, autonomy, and a wide range of transferable skills to add to their portfolio. These skills may include intuitive reasoning, people skills, interpersonal skills, and a sense of humor.
Career Strategies: Learn good communication skills, have a positive attitude, be willing to cross-train, and develop people skills.

Workplace Trends

HITTING THE WALL

If you haven't received a job offer yet, this can be a very discouraging time. You may start doubting your worth and wonder if you'll ever get a job. Everyone goes through periods of doubt and even moments of despair. Being turned down is part of most job searches. Downsizing is occurring at the biggest and best companies. Corporate America is cutting back, and this means fewer jobs and fewer career opportunities. Entry-level jobs are often the hardest hit.

Instead of getting discouraged, broaden your job search.

Scaling the Wall

Scaling the Wall

Research indicates that the more job-search strategies you use, the more you network, and the more companies you contact, the greater your chances for finding a job.

Increase your odds by applying to small companies. According to the Small Business Administration, small to midsized companies make up 99.76 percent of American businesses. Small companies are creating thousands of new jobs.

Taking a job in a small company can also be a smart long-term career move. In a small company, you have an opportunity to learn a variety of new skills, work closely with people from various departments, get involved in more projects, take on more responsibilities, and gain a broader view of business.

The Knockout Factor

- Failure to continue self-assessment.
- Relying on memory for records.
- Failure to continue networking.
- Failure to write thank-you notes.
- Limiting your job-search effort.

The Success Factor

- Continue a self-assessment program.
- Keep organized, detailed written records.
- Follow up on all contacts.
- Write thank-you notes.
- Expand your job search effort to include small and large companies.

PROBLEM SOLVING AT WORK

Problem Solving

Mario has an advanced degree from a prestigious engineering school, good grades, key leadership activities, and impressive references. He followed a focused job-search strategy; carefully completed his self-assessment; and created an active network, an effective resumé, and cover letters. Mario only applied to large impressive companies. He assumed that with his qualifications it would be easy to get a top job at a major company. After being turned down twice, he applied to a small company and was promptly offered a good job. The salary is not as high as he expected, but the opportunities for advancement are excellent.

Mario's decision: Should he accept a job at a small company or hold out for a job at a major, prestigious firm?

1. Have I clearly stated the problem? Should I accept the job at a small company, or should I keep applying to large, prestigious firms.

Define problem: I want to work for a good company in a job that uses my skills and achievements and where I can advance professionally.

What: What company will best reflect my goals and objectives?

Who: Whom should I talk to?

When: When should I accept a job?

Where: Where do I want to work? Should I apply to small as well as large companies?

2. Do I have enough information? Do I have all the information I need to make a decision? Have I researched the benefits of working for a small company?

3. Can I make the decision by myself? What resources are available to help me make a better decision? Have I talked with a career counselor, my advisor, my instructors, people in the same field, and professionals in small companies?

4. Have I brainstormed alternatives? What other methods are available? Should I continue to apply to large and small companies until the offer is finalized?

5. Have I looked at likely consequences? If I take the position at the small company, what are my chances of job success? What are the consequences if I turn the offer down?

6. Have I identified all the resources and tools needed? Have I researched the resources available? Am I knowledgable of the past performance of the small company, training programs, new products, growth projections, and so on?

7. Have I developed and implemented an action plan? Have I designed an action plan that will help me make sound decisions or am I operating on assumptions about large and small companies?

8. Have I identified the best solution and done everything possible to ensure success? Have I made a decision using critical thinking and creativity? Am I committed to making the decision a success?

9. Have I assessed the results? Have I evaluated my decision to see if it is working? Have I assessed my progress, work satisfaction, and long-term career goals?

10. Have I modified the plan, if necessary? What adjustments could I make that would make my decision more successful?

Follow-Up Strategies

- Reassess the success of the interview.
- Follow up with thank-you notes.
- Follow up with phone calls.
- Follow up with good record keeping.
- Continue to network.
- Negotiate the best possible salary.
- Find out the expectations and essential details of the job.

Follow-Up Checklist   Yes   No

1. **Assessment of interview:**
   Followed up on interview assessment?
   Followed up on job-search goals?

2. **Thank-you notes:**
   Wrote thank-you notes?

3. **Networking:**
   Followed up on contacts?

4. **Resumé:**
   Up to date?
   Followed up after sending?

5. **Cover letter:**
   Followed up on letters?

6. **Interviewing:**
   Scheduled and followed up on interviews?

7. **Negotiation:**
   Followed up on salary and benefits?

8. **Reevaluate if necessary?**

9. **Adjusted, if necessary?**

CHAPTER 8

Strategies and Habits for First-Year Job Success

Introduction

A new job presents an exciting opportunity for a better salary, and professional growth. Your first few months can also set the tone for your career at the company. As in the job interview, first impressions are very important!

There are basic strategies that can help you succeed in your new job. Of these strategies, a positive attitude and effective listening skills are the most important. Be enthusiastic, but follow the company's policies and procedures to the letter. Ask questions and listen attentively to your supervisor and co-workers. Make certain you have a clear understanding of your responsibilities, expectations, and limits. Your first year on the job can set the stage for your entire career and you should take advantage of this honeymoon period.

—

Learning Objectives

In Chapter 8, you will learn

- The importance of the first year on the job.

- Success strategies and positive habits.

- How to manage your career.

- The best strategies for getting promoted.

- How to prepare for the changing world of work.

The Importance of the First Year

OK, you've signed the contract; assembled clean, neat, and appropriate clothes for the job; and celebrated getting the job you want. Now it is crucial to follow a path to advancement and success. The first year is a critical transitional time and can make or break your career. You are no longer a student, but are not yet a member of the seasoned professionals. During this orientation period, your supervisors and co-workers will be evaluating you to see how well you adapt to the job routine. The question will be, Did we make a mistake or a good choice? Your every action will be watched.

You need to plan and take charge of your first year as carefully as you planned and initiated your job search. You want to develop a reputation for being a competent, responsible, reliable team player who creatively solves problems and uses critical thinking to make decisions. You form this professional image by consistently following positive habits and by demonstrating skills, good personal characteristics, and the highest standards of ethics.

Learn the Corporate Culture

Every organization has a climate of norms or values that define acceptable behavior. These unwritten rules are almost never discussed but are very real. For example, at some organizations, it is understood that you can call the supervisors by their first names, date other employees, send jokes on E-mail, or wear jeans on Friday. At other organizations, these practices would not be tolerated. It is critical that you learn the corporate culture and understand how you are expected to behave. Keep your eyes open, listen, and ask questions. When in doubt, keep your behavior and appearance professional and conservative.

Observe and Listen

During the first few months, observe and listen more and talk less. This is especially important when it comes to jokes and gossip. A standard rule that will save you embarrassment and career setback is this: Don't take part in gossip. It is never apparent who has the real power in any organization or who is related to or good friends with whom. During the first few months it's better to observe and listen nonjudgmentally. Listen to but don't join in on office gossip. Watch colleagues and observe how things are done. You want to fit into the culture, and this takes time and patience. Some people make the mistake of coming into a new job eager to share their feelings and opinions. They want to show their boss and co-workers how creative and smart they are, so they suggest major changes, criticize established procedures, and love telling people the "right" way to do things. Their attitude says, "How did you manage before I joined this company?"

Don't be a show-off or a know-it-all. Even if you have some great new ideas for how to make the company run better, take time to know the company before you try to impress people with your clever and creative mind. Give yourself a few months to study and ask questions. Take time to listen and observe. The more you know about the work environment, the product, the competition, the corporate culture, office politics, your boss, your clients, and your customers, the easier it will be to offer really sound solutions. Making a big splash, becoming too familiar, and trying too hard to impress rarely work and can ruin a career.

Here are a few questions to help you assess the corporate culture:

- What are the basic procedures in this office?
- What problems keep the company from being more efficient and effective?
- Who really has the power and knowledge?
- Who uses critical thinking to make decisions?
- Who confronts problems directly and solves them?
- Who avoids problems until a crisis occurs?
- Who pulls together the team, and who is highly visible?
- What office games are going on? Are certain people excluded from meetings?
- Who likes to spread rumors and gossip? Who runs to the boss to tattle?
- Whose ideas are listened to and acted upon?
- Does someone steal ideas or take the credit for the work of others?
- Whose doors are open, and where do you go for support?
- Are resources and assistance given to help employees meet their goals?
- Is teamwork encouraged; or are game playing, suspicion, and rumors allowed?
- What behavior gets rewarded: cooperation and direct communication, or hidden messages, power games, and one-upmanship?
- Were you hired over someone who wanted a promotion?
- What were some new ideas that worked in the past?
- How do people get recognized at this organization?
- Do you know office procedures? Whom do you notify if you have a meeting, doctor's appointment, or if you are ill? Do you earn comp time for overtime?
- What is the office policy regarding dating and socializing among employees?

Dating

Dating is one of those sensitive areas that varies from company to company. Follow the conservative rule of taking time to get to know the corporate culture, and don't get overly friendly with anyone for a few months. If you decide dating is acceptable between co-workers in different departments, be very discreet and professional. Leave your personal life at home.

A supervisor should never date or room with a subordinate. Even though the supervisor may be very fair, others could perceive favoritism. You don't have to leave your personality at the office door, but in general, overly flirtatious behavior will undermine your credibility and open you up to office gossip and rumors.

Create Positive Work Attitudes and a Polished Image

Your attitude at the beginning of a job is the most critical factor for success. Be upbeat, optimistic, alert, and attentive. Everyone goes through career setbacks and disappointments. As we've discussed throughout this book, positive habits are thoughts and actions you have practiced consistently and that you do without thinking. Therefore, it is important to develop a habit of being positive. Professionals bounce back and look for the good side of every situation. If you are enthusiastic, positive, and motivated, you will outshine the average employee.

Professional Image

Create a professional and positive image. Give up your student casual dress and make certain you are dressed in a neat, clean, and businesslike manner. Review the guidelines in Chapter 5 on putting together a professional business wardrobe. Occasionally take a hard look at yourself in the mirror and periodically assess if you look like a polished professional on your way up.

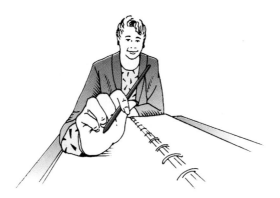

Be a Lifelong Learner

Learning new skills and getting additional training to enhance your abilities will be key for success. Peter Drucker, author of *Management: Tasks, Responsibilities, Practices,* writes that there are three conditions for excellent work: productive work, feedback, and continual learning.

Don't wait for the company to send you to school. Determine your needs and ask about the company's training program. If they don't have one, sign up for classes at a local college. Put a high priority on learning new skills and on personal growth, and professional development. Learn new software technology and improve interpersonal and writing skills.

Continue to Learn New Technical and Job Skills

Take classes and advance training. Read books, professional journals, and management articles. Learning new computer and telecommunications skills can make you very valuable to the company. Cross-learn other jobs. Take an interest in learning sales, marketing, production, and various other tasks and procedures around the company. Study the competition. What are their strengths and weaknesses?

Improve Your Verbal Communication and Listening Skills

The higher up you go in any organization, the more important communication skills are to your effectiveness. Mean what you say, and say what you mean. All companies value the employee who can speak in a concise, clear, and direct manner. Learn to get your points across effectively and give effective speeches and outstanding presentations. Join Toastmasters or take a college class and practice often. As with any other skill, you must commit yourself to learning the basics and then practice with diligence.

A large part of communication involves listening. Be an active listener who listens for understanding and for the intent of the speaker. Paraphrase what the speaker has said so you know you both understand. Never interrupt others. Be patient and allow them to finish before you make your points.

Learn Good Written Communication Skills

It is vital that you demonstrate the ability to write in a clear, concise, and direct manner. Practice writing and take classes. Collect good memos and reports to use as models.

Learn Problem-Solving and Decision-Making Skills

Learn about the problems and concerns of the company and brainstorm solutions. Learn from your experiences and from others. Listen to how people you admire have handled problems and made decisions.

Being known as a person who can solve problems and make sound decisions will give you an edge in advancing your career. Every job involves problem solving and decision making. You will want to find out the perimeters of your accountability. Study problems in your group so that when the time comes you will have the information to offer solutions. Employees who see change and problems as challenges to overcome and opportunities for growth tend to be more productive and happy. By following a step-by-step procedure, the same one we've been using to make decisions in the job-search process, you will be known as a person who is a creative problem solver and who uses critical thinking to make decisions.

Problem-Solving Strategies

1. State the problem.
2. Gather information.
3. Brainstorm creative solutions.
4. State the consequences of each solution.
5. Clarify your purpose. What results do you want?
6. Select the best alternative.
7. Review the pros and cons of the best alternative.
8. Act on the best alternative.
9. Evaluate based on critical thinking.
10. Adjust as necessary.

When you have a problem, come up with several solutions. Choose the one you think is best and try to determine the likely consequences. Your boss will know that you have good problem-solving and critical-thinking skills, but are not too arrogant to ask for advice or approval when necessary.

You can have competent job skills, technical knowledge, and be committed, but success will elude you if you don't have a positive attitude and the ability to work effectively with others. Employers want to know if you have confidence, enthusiasm, perseverance, health and energy, intelligence, maturity, diligence, a positive attitude, initiative, creativity, and the ability to relate and work with different people.

- Ask for feedback. When starting new projects, get advice. Review how you have handled projects and problems in the past. What have you learned about yourself? Ask for feedback from others and be open to growth.
- Take charge of your career. Set goals for learning new skills, assess your progress, and map out a plan of action.

Develop Personal Qualities and People Skills

Employers always value people who have people skills. They place a great premium on the ability to work effectively with people.

Personal qualities that are valued include

Honesty	Integrity	Sensitivity
Compassion	Fairness	Devotion to the truth
Commitment	Concern for others	Trustworthiness
Courtesy	Respect	Courage
Loyalty	Openness to change	

Ethics and Integrity

Business ethics requires that you not only follow obvious moral laws such as not stealing from the company or lying, but that you conduct yourself with absolute integrity in daily actions. Nothing is as important as your reputation! While ethics are a code or system of moral principles, integrity refers to the adherence of your individual principles of honest and moral character. For example, accepting gifts from your clients may be legal and even acceptable under the ethical code of your office, but your own sense of integrity may not allow it or you may be faced with a situation where your supervisor says it is Ok to omit certain information, but you may consider the omissions to be lying and the action would not fit in with your sense of moral character or integrity. Having integrity and business ethics means you are honest, aboveboard, and straight with people. You don't lie or stretch the truth just to make a sale or impress others. You keep your word and honor your agreements. You admit when you are wrong and never blame others or cover up when you make a mistake. Ethical people take responsibility for their actions and behaviors. They never intentionally hurt other people and are aware of the consequences of their decisions. They are critical thinkers who make decisions based on fact but also consider the human factor.

Like ethics, civility is the cornerstone of a supportive and productive climate. Treat everyone with respect and kindness. Profanity, sexual or racial remarks, gossip, one-upmanship, and tactless behavior do not belong in the workplace.

Assess your personal qualities and make a commitment to follow the highest ideals in all areas of your life. Be truthful, reliable, responsible, and diligent in the effective use of company resources.

Before you make a remark or a decision, ask yourself these questions:

1. Is this action legal? Does it comply with the company's policies, procedures, and values? If my parents, spouse, or child were here, would I say or do this?

2. How would I feel later? How would my actions or behavior make me feel about myself?

3. How would others see me? If my actions were written in a news article and put on the front page of the paper, what impression would the public, my family, my co-workers, and my friends have of me?

4. Is this action fair?

5. Is this action true?

6. Would this action be hurtful? Would this remark or action cause someone to be hurt or embarrassed?

Take Responsibility for Your Actions

You will make mistakes. No one expects you to be perfect, but they do expect you to be responsible and honest. No one likes a whiner. When mistakes happen, don't justify, blame, or cover up; just take responsibility apologize once, and go on.

Take responsibility for making the company more successful. Never say, "This isn't my job." or "Sorry, I only work here. I don't make the policy." Notice small things that can be done and take steps to create a really outstanding company.

Take responsibility for your community. Get involved and contribute your talents and time. Join a worthwhile community project or board and gain visibility through community service so that people in the community, company, and industry know who you are.

Be Known as a Doer

Get organized and do first things first. Some people talk a good game but don't produce results. Be results-oriented. Get projects done and done on time. Follow through on commitments and practice good organizational and time management skills that will help you be more successful. Managing your time better can help you:

- Be more effective at work.
- Enjoy your job.
- Improve your health.
- Lower your stress.
- Have more time for family, friends, and hobbies.
- Increase your self-esteem and sense of competency.

Assess your Time and Resources

Take stock of your day. What are your time wasters? Are you putting a lot of time into low-priority items or areas that do not produce results? Could your office, equipment, or scheduling be rearranged to help you be more productive? Are you trying to work hard and think creatively during low-energy times? Are you opening the mail and doing mundane tasks during high-energy time? Assess how organized and effective you are.

Invest in the resources and equipment that can help you be more effective at home and in the office. A new computer, software, printer, organizer, answering machine, fax, or car phone may help you increase productivity.

Get Organized

Take time to get organized. Sometimes, it is essential to work Saturday morning or over lunch a few days to get yourself organized. Make certain that files are in the right place and that you have the necessary data for your projects. Look at the arrangement of your office. Could it be set up more efficiently?

Don't Overlook The Little Things

- Arriving on time or a few minutes before a meeting or appointment begins is important.
- Do first things first and respond quickly to requests for information.
- Take careful notes and document deadlines.
- Write all appointments down.
- Make certain you meet all deadlines.
- Review procedures in a small group.
- Project the most likely consequence of a decision.
- Assess and adjust when necessary.
- Be a good follow-through person.
- Write notes to yourself.
- Return phone calls.
- Call customers back.
- Write action steps to projects.
- Follow up on all details.
- Do the unpleasant things that you tend to put off.
- Remind team members, tactfully, to finish projects.
- Don't make promises you can't keep.

Responsibility and dependability are two attributes of a promotable person. Demonstrate that you have learned from your mistakes and that you have the resiliency to pick yourself up and succeed.

Use the Power of Teamwork

Too many people think they must be the corporate star and want to work alone. Most companies, however, require a team effort. Participate in group projects and activities. It is critical that you develop a team-player mentality and learn to work effectively with a variety of people. Working as a team member can enhance your productivity, foster creative ideas, and help you solve problems and make decisions. Learn to have a positive attitude even when you are working with difficult people. Appreciate differences in people and bring out their best qualities. Don't expect people to be perfect. Everyone makes mistakes. Accept people and look for the best in them. Most people will act as you expect them to.

Be Visible and Action-Oriented

Increase Your Visibility

You will not be valued if you aren't visible. People need to know what you are doing and contributing. If no one knows you are doing great things, you'll never get promoted. Employees who keep their nose to the grindstone and never come out of their office usually don't get promoted. Increase your visibility by volunteering for new projects, giving presentations, or writing an article for a trade publication. Don't kid yourself that if you are patient and work hard, promotions and salary increases will be automatic. Workplace decisions are often not fair or equitable. Let top management know what you have accomplished. Get involved in the company.

Be confident and don't undermine your sense of worth by saying, "Oh, it was really nothing." You need not be arrogant or inflated, but quietly enhance your visibility by speaking up for yourself. It is important to know and appreciate your own worth and accomplishments and speak about them in a direct manner.

Have lunch with different people from various areas of the company. Volunteer to be on committees for office projects or to organize social events. This will demonstrate that you work well as a team member and will increase your visibility with the company. If the opportunity should arise, volunteer for projects or offer to chair meetings. Remember, it is important to increase your visibility among your co-workers as well as gain visibility with your supervisors.

Ask your boss for more exposure. Ask if you can give speeches, make presentations, arrange meetings, and take on new projects. As we discussed in Chapter 2 on networking, find a boss, mentor, or role model who is committed to your development and who will help you enhance your visibility.

Give It All You've Got the First Year

You not only have to work smart, you have to work hard and put in extra hours at a new job. Come into work early, leave later than most, and put in some night and weekend hours. Really commit yourself to the company and show loyalty, excitement, and old-fashioned hard work. There is a certain focus that occurs when you throw your whole heart into your job. Give it all you've got from day one. Be on time to all meetings, be alert, and be actively involved. Volunteer for jobs that no one else wants to tackle. Make certain your desk is cleared off at the end of the day and you've spent a few minutes reviewing the next day's priorities.

Paying Your Dues

As a new employee, you may be asked to perform many tasks: running errands, making coffee, taking notes, making copies, fixing a broken tape recorder, setting up a room for presentations. You may get the most undesirable office, equipment, and assignments. Don't let your ego get in the way. Every job has its unpleasant task, and as you demonstrate your willingness to do whatever needs to be done to achieve your objectives, you will move up in the company. It is expected that new employees pay their dues. Offer to stuff envelopes, take packages to the mail room, be a greeter at receptions, and work some nights and weekends. Volunteer to help with new assignments or projects—even out of your area (with the approval of your boss). This is a much better way to learn about a new company than just asking questions or reading materials. You will also be visible, get to know a lot of people, and be known as a doer who is not afraid to roll up your sleeves.

Continue to Network

Networking is vital for making contacts and creating a professional support base. You can utilize contacts in your network to help solve problems, to gain advice and guidance, and to gain and give support.

Keep an updated resumé in your file at all times. It is important that you have a well-organized, professional, concise, and attractive resumé to enhance your marketability. Even if you are not looking for a new job at this time, you need to know that you are marketable.

We've discussed how important networking is for professional survival and for advancement. Networking can also boost your visibility. You will find that you gain leadership skills and visibility by getting actively involved in professional organizations. Send articles to professional journals, offer to be on their editorial board and planning committees. In a sense, you are managing your own image and career development. Networking can help you stay visible, knowledgeable, current, and on top of job opportunities in the workplace.

Getting Promoted

Create an Effective Relationship with Your Supervisor

Most employees know the importance of working effectively with others and managing their careers. Few relationships, however, will be as critical as the one you develop with your boss. You will want to develop effective communication, create trust, and support the people you work with. Your supervisor is the one person who is responsible for rewarding your performance, helping you to be more visible, and promoting you to a new position. Therefore, creating a good working relationship with your boss is a key skill in managing your career. Creating a solid work relationship means working together to solve the company's problems and developing mutual respect and trust. From day one, ask your boss which assignments and job duties are most important and which decisions should be discussed together. You want to be seen as a self-starter, but you don't want to overstep your bounds of authority.

Use the following guidelines to build a positive working relationship with your supervisor:

- Set mutual goals and clarify expectations.
- Keep your boss informed.
- Understand both your and your boss's duties, concerns, projects, and goals.
- Assess both your and your boss's strengths and weaknesses. How can you support your supervisor?
- Understand and respect your boss's personal style.
- Maintain clear, direct, and honest communication. Ask for feedback.
- Acknowledge and praise good work accomplished by your supervisor and co-workers.
- Understand the performance review system and evaluate yourself. Make certain you have set goals and deadlines and have recorded your progress.
- Keep an accurate record on your calendar of meetings and of dates projects are due and submitted.
- Keep a file of memos sent, performance evaluations, a list of achievements, and letters of appreciation.

The Performance Review

Performance review systems vary from company to company, but few are excellent or motivational. Many companies use a standard form and conduct a performance review once a year. Therefore, it is up to you to manage your own performance review and career growth. You don't need to wait to be formally evaluated. Prepare for your appraisal so you can make it as accurate, pleasant, and helpful as possible. Be realistic, but expect the best. To prepare, use the following guidelines.

1. Review your formal job description. Update it when you take on more assignments and projects. Do you exceed requirements for your job? What job assignments could you take on that would enhance your position? What relationships could you develop that would help you do your job better? What new skills could you learn that would improve your performance?

2. Get a copy of the company's performance review. Ask personnel for a copy of the standard performance review document the company uses. Review the criteria and make certain you understand what you will be rated on. Most appraisals look at several areas.

a. **Objective results.**
What goals and duties do you perform which you measure the results? How can you assess your bottom-line results in quantifiable terms? Keep accurate records of production, sales quotas, cost budgets, number of customers helped, and so on.

b. **Behavior.**
Do you put forth the effort to achieve? Do you appear confident and professional? Do you handle stress well?

c. **Attitude.**
Do you have a positive attitude? Do you show enthusiasm for your work?

d. **Teamwork.**
Do you work well with others? Are you willing to chip in and do more than your share of the work to get a project completed? Do you need to be a star and get the credit, or can you focus on team effort?

e. **Deadlines.**
Do you meet deadlines?

f. **Office policies and procedures.**
Do you come to work on time and work hard all day? Do you always let people know where you are when you're away from your desk? Do you observe office procedures concerning overtime, travel expenses, time off, vacations, and so forth?

Below is a sample performance review form.

PERFORMANCE REVIEW

NAME_____ POSITION_____ DIV./DEPT._____ DATE OF APPOINTMENT_____

FROM_____TO_____Return To Personnel Office Before_____
(RATING PERIOD)

Unsatisfactory	Satisfactory	SECTION A	Not Rated	
		Rate only those factors that apply to this position. Immediate Supervisor must check each appropriate factor in the proper columns. Additional factors may be added as appropriate to the position.		SECTION B Record job STRENGTHS & superior performance incidents.
		1. Observance of work hours		
		2. Attendance		
		3. Public contacts		
		4. Employee contacts		
		5. Communication with others		SECTION C Record specific work performance DEFICIENCIES or job behavior requiring improvement or correction.
		6. Knowledge of work		
		7. Work judgments		
		8. Planning & organizing		
		9. Job skill level		
		10. Quality of work		
		11. Acceptable work volume		
		12. Meeting deadlines		
		13. Accepts responsibility		
		14. Accepts direction		
		15. Operation & care of equipment		SECTION D Record specific GOALS or IMPROVEMENT PROGRAMS to be undertaken during next evaluation period.
		16. Initiative & creativity		
		17. Learning ability		
		18. Work station appearance		
		19. Safety practices		
		20. Accepts change		
		21. Effectiveness under stress		
		22. Work coordination		SECTION E Do you recommend retention or termination at this time?
		23.		SECTION F This employee is eligible for Merit Salary Adjustment on_____ In my judgment, the employee's job performance:
		24.		_____ meets the level of quality and quantity expected. I recommend that the employee be granted a merit salary adjustment.
		25.		_____ does not meet the level of quality and quantity expected. I recommend that the employee not be granted a merit salary adjustment at this time, and have so informed the employee.
		Any unsatisfactory rating must be explained in Section C		
		For employees who supervise others:		
		26. Planning and organizing		SECTION G The last position description on file in this office is dated_____ (Date)
		27. Scheduling & coordinating		Is this description still accurate?_____
		28. Training and instructing		We have no position description for this position. ☐
		29. Productivity		I certify that this report represents my best judgment. RATER:
		30. Evaluating subordinates		
		31. Judgments & decisions		_____ (Rater's Signature) (Title) (Date)
		32. Leadership skills		
		33. Operational skills		DEPARTMENT HEAD/DEAN:
		34. Supervisory control		_____ (Signature) (Title) (Date)
		35. Compliance with affirmative action rules		
		ROUTING: White – Personnel Canary– Department Pink – Employee		EMPLOYEE: I certify that this report has been discussed with me. I understand my signature does not necessarily indicate agreement. Comment: _____ (Employee's Signature)_____ (Date)_____

3. Assess your performance. Make certain your work is up to your own and your supervisor's standard of excellence. Develop professional credibility. You want to achieve a reputation for competence that is acknowledged by your co-workers and your supervisor. Have you met your goals in measurable ways? Compare your evaluation of your performance with the standard performance review form. What items could be seen as weaknesses? Do you have measurable results? What have you accomplished that is outstanding? In what areas do you think you need to improve?

4. Establish good communication with your supervisor. Set up a time to review your performance with your supervisor on a regular basis. After projects, make certain you have feedback from your supervisor about how you could improve. Make certain that letters of appreciation from customers go into your file. Ask your supervisor what you can do to improve.

5. Action plan. Develop an action plan for how you are going to improve. Do you need to develop new skills? What kinds of training programs or classes can you sign up for? Do you want to go on for a degree or just learn new skills? How can you prepare for greater responsibility?

Manage Your Performance Reviews

Throughout this book, the benefit factor has been stressed. You will want to continue to find ways to add value to the organization. In fact, you should ask yourself regularly, "How do I demonstrate value to the company?" One way to monitor your contribution is to use the performance review form to evaluate your progress.

Part of managing your career is to take control of your performance reviews. Too often people avoid or dread performance reviews. Your performance review, however, provides the feedback you need to assess your strengths and concerns and set goals.

Assess Your Job Description

Begin by reviewing your job description. What functions do you perform that add value to the company? How would you rank this value? Make certain you have a detailed job description. You should know what is expected of you and what specific skills, functions, and personal qualities are required or desired for your position. Determine what skills and qualities can be measured and how you can determine results.

Ask for Feedback

Tell your supervisor you want to be told of concerns and problems *when they occur*. Stress that you cannot grow professionally or change your behavior if you are not aware of concerns until the yearly performance review.

Set Your Goals and Objectives

Usually, you will set your goals and objectives with your boss. Even if your boss doesn't give you guidance, you can develop your goals and objectives based on your job description and shared discussions with your supervisor and work team members. Send a copy to your supervisor and ask if these are agreeable expectations.

Create Your Own Evaluation System

Conduct your own performance review by setting goals and initiating a time frame using a matrix system, such as the one in Exercise 8.1.

1. Determine the functions that you perform that are of value to the company.

2. Assign a value of this function to the company. "A" being most valuable and so on.

3. Determine the necessary steps you would take to translate this function into a series of action steps.

4. Ask customers, co-workers, professional peers, and supervisors to review your actions. Feedback can only help you succeed.

What barriers have you encountered, and what changes occurred after setting your goals? If you met your goals on time, what factors and resources helped you? If you didn't meet your goals, what factors and barriers got in your way? Adjust your goals based upon the data you have collected. Adjust and modify your goals and objectives for next year.

Having measurable objectives and results concerning your performance and a systematic plan of action in hand will help you assess your own progress and set future objectives. You will be taking control of your career and not just reacting to feedback from your supervisor.

Review your job description and the main functions of your job. Review the goals you have set for the first six months and indicate how you will measure outcomes. Determine how you can evaluate each stage of the process to help you produce the results you want. Review the company's performance review form and add criteria you think important for achieving the results you want.

For functions 1 and 2, we've listed the steps needed to improve performance in each function area. In addition, we've described how improvement can be measured. For a job you've had in the past, choose three functions and list steps for improvement and criteria to measure results, filling in the matrix below.

Function	Value	Steps	Measure Results
1. Meeting customer needs.	A	• Return phone calls. • Provide status reports. • Assess input from customers. • Clarify customer needs.	• Positive feed back. • Increased business. • Improved rapport. • Positive reports.
2. Keeping commitments to customers.	A	• Create a follow-up file. • Establish a to-do list. • Set written goals. • Monitor progress of each phase.	• Increased productivity. • Reputation for keeping agreements. • Customers will call you more often. • Positive responses and letters of recognition.
3. _____ _____	___ ___	_____ _____ _____	_____ _____ _____
4. _____ _____	___ ___	_____ _____ _____	_____ _____ _____
5. _____ _____		_____ _____ _____	_____ _____ _____

During your career, assess how well your job meets your needs. Put a check next to what you have and what you want in a job. The number of matches indicates if your job is a good match for you at this time.

Job Factor	What You Have	What You Want
1. Career advancement.	_____	_____
2. Personal growth.	_____	_____
3. Independence.	_____	_____
4. Opportunity to learn.	_____	_____
5. Good pay.	_____	_____
6. Good benefits.	_____	_____
7. Travel.	_____	_____
8. Flexible hours.	_____	_____
9. Job security.	_____	_____
10. Allows creative problem solving.	_____	_____
11. Challenging.	_____	_____
12. Allows me to use my skills.	_____	_____
13. Good working relationships with co-workers.	_____	_____
14. High visibility.	_____	_____
15. Opportunity to work as a team.	_____	_____
16. Involves education and training.	_____	_____
17. Good relationship with supervisor.	_____	_____
18. Good mentor relationship.	_____	_____
19. A sense of contributing to the world.	_____	_____

Be Careful of Job Hopping

Throughout your career, you will want to continue to assess your interests, skills, job satisfaction, and performance. If after evaluating your job, you believe you've made a big mistake or if you think your company is involved in unethical activities, look for a new job. However, resist the urge to job hop at the first sign of dissatisfaction. You can damage your career by having too many jobs in a short period. There will always be something you don't like about every job. In addition, your first full-time job is a big transition. Just getting used to long hours that are usually not flexible is a major adjustment. Consider your options carefully before you quit.

THE BENEFIT FACTOR

The Benefit Factor

You can have great ideas, a solid education, and team skills, but if you don't have high energy, success will pass you by. People who succeed have the personal energy and health to work hard, cope with stress, and maintain a demanding schedule when deadlines approach. Regular exercise is important for good health, maintaining your ideal weight, increasing your energy, reducing stress, and creating a sense of well-being. Find an activity you like to do—jogging, walking, aerobics, bicycling—and commit to doing it regularly. Parking the car a 10- or 15-minute walk from work or walking during lunch hour works for some people.

A new job demands longer hours. However, it is also critical that you think about balance. Obviously, you want to work hard, especially during the first year, but you also need to learn when you have reached the point where you could burn out. You will have more job success and greater marketability if you show you have learned to balance your personal and professional life. Taking care of yourself physically and mentally is critical for job success. You will be healthier, have more energy, and have a valuable job skill when you learn how to cope successfully with stress. You will have much more to contribute to the company if you have personal energy and vitality that comes from health and stamina.

Leaving a Job

Don't Burn Your Bridges

At some point in almost everyone's career, it is necessary to leave a job. As mentioned earlier, today's workers can expect to change jobs at least four times. There are, of course, many reasons for choosing to leave a job. Your spouse may have relocated through his or her job to another part of the country. You may have heard about another job that seems like a real career booster, is more challenging, or looks like a better fit with your talents and your career goals. Your interests may have changed enough to make your current job seem less desirable. In some cases, the time frame for promotion at your current company may not suit your expectations.

When the time comes to leave your job, do so with grace and professionalism. Don't burn your bridges by leaving on a negative note, even if you haven't enjoyed working with some of your colleagues.

Continue to act like a professional even as you clean out your desk. Negative comments always get back to people and you will end up looking bad. In addition, your colleagues may change companies, too, and you may even find yourself working with them again someday. Always treat others with civility and respect even if they are being unreasonable.

Do your best to leave your job in good shape. Give enough notice and finish major projects. Leave details of your assignments and let other people in the office know what you have been working on. Let them know that you can be reached by phone if there are questions. In short, be responsible.

One way to ensure a smooth exit is to write a clear and thoughtful letter of resignation that acknowledges your supervisor and thanks him or her for the chance to work at the organization and learn new skills. Again, be complimentary and gracious—this isn't the time to vent frustrations.

A sample letter of resignation is shown below.

January 17, 1995

Mr. Walter Knapp
Director of Sales and Marketing
Bechtel Information Services, Inc.
P.O. Box 1372
Savannah, Georgia 31402

Dear Mr. Knapp:

Please accept this letter as my official notice of resignation. I have accepted a position with Abbott International as Field Supervisor for Sales. I will begin my new assignment February 1.

It has been a pleasure to work with you the past three years. I have appreciated your continual support, guidance, and unfailing good humor. I have learned a great deal about customer service from your example and commitment. I plan to continue making customer satisfaction a top priority in my new position.

I wish you continual success.

Sincerely,

Barry

Barry T. Kason
723 Pine Street
Savannah, Georgia 31402

Send a note to your boss and co-workers, thanking them for having been given the opportunity to work with them. After a few weeks on your new job, call and see how things are going and if they have any questions on your projects.

THE REVOLUTIONARY WORKPLACE

Key: Change and Adaptation

Shifts in the economy and corporate buyouts may result in layoffs, mergers, downsizing, forced retirement, and job changes. The workplace of tomorrow will be an entirely different place. Flexibility and the ability to learn new skills will be key. Even though career professionals know it is important to adapt to change, many people resist change and fear going beyond their comfort zone. It is important to change your perception of security and develop ways to gain the skills, personal qualities, and education that will make you more marketable and give you a sense of competency. As you grow professionally, it will be even more important to be aware of job trends. Here are a few trends that are changing the nature of the workplace.

Workplace Trends

Decentralized Problem Solving

The computer age has placed valuable information, once the domain of top management, in the hands of all workers. The entry-level clerk can access information at the flip of a laptop. Self-direction is replacing the old mode of only doing what you are told to do. A store manager, a few years ago, was told what products would be sent from headquarters. Now data is customized and received via laptops through reports generated at headquarters. Each morning, local managers can access information on sales, profits, new products, and trends. This new technology, plus the elimination of layers of middle managers, means that people closest to the customers will be making decisions. Employees will enjoy more autonomy, greater responsibility, and more control over what they do.

Training and Education

One important job trend is the increasing importance of education and training. The amount of available information, and the ways we can retrieve it, is growing in leaps and bounds. Adaptable employees need to know how to stay on top. If you want to go into management or supervision, it is even more important to continue to learn new skills and to keep up on new trends.

1. **Get more education and training.** Keep yourself up-to-date by taking classes at a local college, attending training programs and conferences, and keeping active in professional associations.

2. **Learn new skills.** Skills in computers, grant writing, negotiations, foreign language, fiscal management, marketing, innovative delivery systems, customer relations, and human relations will make you more marketable.

3. **Learn and consistently practice good habits.** Qualities such as enthusiasm and a positive attitude, tolerance, perseverance, and hard work are vital for job success.

4. **Cross-training.** Learn other jobs at your company. Volunteer to take on new projects. Ask how other departments do certain jobs. Create a booklet of policies and procedures.

Cultural Diversity

The workplace of the future will be more diverse and reflect the changing national racial profile. In 1990, 84 percent of Americans were white. Census Bureau projections indicate that by the year 2020, the proportion of Americans that are white will drop to 78 percent. Hispanics, African Americans, and Asians will make up at least a third of the population. Border states, such as California, will reflect an even greater racial mix. Minorities and women will be entering the labor force in greater numbers. In fact, over half of all workers entering the workplace during the next decade will be immigrants or the children of immigrants. It will be increasingly important to pay more attention to cultural and gender diversity in the workplace. The successful employee must be able to work with people of different ethnic and racial backgrounds, genders, ages, able-bodiedness, and lifestyle preferences.

Workplace Trends

Diversity Strategies

1. **Value differences.** It will be important to not only *tolerate* differences, but learn to *value* and *appreciate* diversity.

2. **Take an interest.** Learn about other cultures, religions, and races. Attend workshops and be aware that people learn, solve problems, and relate to others in different ways.

3. **Create an open mind-set.** Be tolerant and get into the habit of understanding other people. See things from different points of view.

4. **Review policies and procedures on diversity.** Make certain that your organization has policies that ensure respect and protect people from discrimination. If not, you may question whether you want to work for an organization that doesn't appear to value diversity. Or you may want to take a leadership role in developing programs, policies, and procedures that help support cultural diversity.

5. **Create diverse work teams.** Look at work teams in your office.fresh A diverse team is necessary to approach problems in creative and ways. Make a commitment to create a climate of respect and understanding.

Sexual Harassment

Sexual harassment is behavior that has a sexual connotation and is unwelcomed, unwanted, and demeaning and creates a hostile or abusive work environment. The U.S. Supreme Court in 1993 ruled that a hostile work environment need not be psychologically injurious but only **reasonably perceived as abusive.** Sexual or cultural harassment is illegal, unnecessary, and destructive in the workforce. It is also costly. Besides expensive legal cost, the work climate suffers from loss of productivity, low morale, and distrust. Managers are responsible for ensuring that appropriate guidelines are established and posted and that they are in compliance with the law. The corporate climate must respect differences in gender, race, culture, and religion. As an employee, you should know company policies and procedures. Does your company follow these general guidelines?

1. **Does the company have a written policy?** Does the company have a posted written policy concerning sexual harassment, describing how to file and the disciplinary actions that may result because of inappropriate behavior?

2. **Is there a designated person?** Has the company assigned a person who is knowledgeable, fair, and approachable to handle complaints concerning sexual harassment?

3. **Is the company in compliance with policies and laws?** Are employee behaviors and work practices in compliance with the policy?

Alcohol and Drug Abuse

Workplace Trends

The effects of alcohol and drug abuse in the workplace can be devastating and staggering.

1. **Know the cost involved.** The National Institute of Drug Abuse has estimated that drug and alcohol abuse cost the U.S. economy over $150 billion every year in lower productivity, medical care, lost wages, higher insurance premiums, and property damages. All employees should be aware that drug and alcohol abuse can cost the company real profit.

2. **Keep up on the laws.** In some states companies are required to provide separate areas for smokers to protect nonsmokers from the harmful effects of second hand smoke. In other states, smoking is prohibited any where in the workplaces. Some companies are reluctant to hire smokers because of the increased health risks of cancer, chronic bronchitis, and emphysema. As an employee, know the laws regarding safe work environments, hiring guidelines, drug testing, and treatment programs.

3. **Get help.** If you have a problem, get help. Employees should know signs to watch for in substance abuse and the resources available for treatment.

AIDS

Employees need to have the facts and accurate information on AIDS in the workplace. Fear and discrimination can be eliminated if facts replace rumors and misinformation. Employees need to know and practice established policies and procedures on how to protect themselves from the virus, especially in high-risk situations.

Career Strategies: Be flexible, able and willing to adapt to change, and sensitive and appreciative of diversity.

HITTING THE WALL

Scaling the Wall

Even if you have a great job, it is often a rude awakening to work long hours every day. Gone are summer vacations, long breaks at Christmas, spring break, and classes that start at 10:00 in the morning. Even if you worked while going to school, you probably had flexible time, breaks, and variety in your schedule. One of the hardest habits for new employees to develop is a strong work ethic. Most jobs require employees to work from 8:00 A.M. to 5:00 P.M. with an hour off for lunch. If you want to be successful, however, you will find that you need to work more hours than what is expected—especially when a deadline is due. Visibility is important. Most young professionals who are successful get to work early, eat lunch with co-workers, stay late, work weekends, travel, and do more than is required.

During the first year it is especially important to establish a strong track record, and that means putting in extra hours and being visible and involved. This can result in exhaustion and stress unless you know how to increase your energy and stamina and balance your life.

Scaling the Wall

Increase your energy.

Starting your day right will help you form positive work habits:

- **Get organized.** The night before, lay out your clothes and put your briefcase and keys by the door. Get up early. Don't get stressed out by being late or looking for lost items.

- **Get plenty of rest.** Get to bed early, at about the same time every night. Give up your late nights and establish a regular routine of sleep so that you are at work not only early, but energized, focused, clear-headed, and enthusiastic.

- **Eat healthy foods.** You can't have energy if your diet is poor. Eat a balanced diet of foods rich in vitamins and fiber, such as whole grains, vegetables, fruits, low-fat milk, and protein. Keep healthy snacks in your desk to help you avoid that tempting doughnut with your coffee break.

- **Get regular exercise.** Nothing increases your energy like exercise. In order to build lasting energy and health, you must get regular, aerobic exercise. Get up early enough to do 10 or 15 minutes of exercise. Take a brisk walk at lunch or instead of a coffee break, or work out in a gym a few times a week. Do yoga or stretching exercises at night to relax.

- **Do something you enjoy every day.** Take time to read for pleasure, visit with friends, write, play sports, and enjoy simple pleasures.

- **Avoid energy downers.** Alcohol, cigarettes, and drugs are depressants and will sap your energy. Too much caffeine will also cause your energy to dip.

- **Use positive images and self-talk.** Visualize yourself as a competent, caring, positive, professional. Mentally walk through your day before you get out of bed. See yourself handling any problem in a calm, positive, and creative matter. Keep a list of affirmations in your desk and say them often. Remember, self-esteem is something you give yourself; it is a habit that you can create through positive self-talk, visualization, learning new skills, and positive habits.

The Knockout Factor	The Success Factor
• Not learning the corporate culture.	• Take time to learn the corporate culture.
• Having a negative attitude and unprofessional image.	• Create a positive attitude and polished image.
• Not learning technical skills.	• Be a lifelong and willing learner.
• Not developing positive habits and personal qualities.	• Develop positive habits and solid personal qualities.
• Not taking charge of your career.	• Take charge of your career.
• Not establishing regular feedback with your boss and co-workers.	• Take charge of your performance reviews and get regular feedback.
• Not being visible.	• Create high visibility.
• Not developing a strong network.	• Develop a strong network.
• Thinking the company owes you a job.	• Realize your job depends on the value you create.

PROBLEM SOLVING AT WORK

Problem Solving

John graduated several years ago with a certificate in architectural drafting and design. He does his job well and is competent, but he hasn't been promoted. John believed that once he got his certificate and performed the duties of his job description, he would automatically get promoted. He knows it is time to reassess his skills, personal qualities, and achievements and to take control of his career. John knows he either has to make himself more visible and valuable at his present job or more marketable for a new job. What would you suggest to help John get take control of his career?

1. Have I clearly stated the problems? Should I accept the way things are, feel lucky to have a job, and wait for a promotion, or should I take active control of my career?

> **Define problem:** I want to advance professionally and yet not "rock the boat."
>
> **What:** What can I do that would help me gain a promotion and be more valuable to the company?
>
> **Who:** Who should I talk to?
>
> **When:** Should I wait for my annual performance review to bring up a promotion?
>
> **Where:** Where do I go to get training, learn new skills, and find out what positions are available?

2. Do I have enough information? Do I have all the information I need to make a decision? Do I know the company's policy for promotions? Am I aware of other positions in the company that would give me valuable experience? Have I researched the benefits of training programs?

3. Can I make the decision by myself? What resources are available to help me make a better decision? Have I talked with a career counselor, my advisor, my instructors, people in the same field, and professionals in the field?

4. Have I brainstormed alternatives? What other methods are available? Could I cross-train with other departments?

5. Have I looked at likely consequences? If I take a more active role in my performance reviews, what are my chances of job success? What are the consequences if I don't get a promotion?

6. Have I identified all the resources and tools needed? Have I researched the resources available? Have I looked into training programs, advanced degrees, special workshops, and classes?

7. Have I developed and implemented an action plan? Have I designed an action plan that will help me make sound decisions, or am I just waiting for my boss to give me a promotion?

8. Have I identified the best solution and done everything possible to ensure success? Have I made a decision using critical thinking and creativity? Am I committed to making the decision a success?

9. Have I assessed the results? Have I evaluated my decision to see if it is working? Have I assessed my progress, work satisfaction, and long-term career goals?

10. Have I modified the plan, if necessary? What adjustments could I make that would help me to be more successful?

First-Year Success Strategies

- Learn the corporate culture.
- Listen, be aware, and ask questions. Be willing to learn.
- Develop positive work habits.
- Improve communication and listening skills.
- Give it all you've got. Work extra hours.
- Create effective work relationships.
- Manage your performance reviews.
- Increase your visibility.
- Continue to network.
- Increase your energy and balance.
- Use the power of teamwork.
- Be professional.
- Take responsibility for your actions.
- Live with absolute integrity.
- Create and maintain a positive attitude.

First-Year Checklist   Yes   No

1. Positive attitude?
2. Understand corporate culture?
3. Professional image?
4. Knowledgeable about company?
5. Learn new skills?
6. Develop solid work relationships?
7. Creative problem solver?
8. Use critical thinking in decision making?
9. Manage performance reviews?
10. Increased visibility?
11. Manage and adapt to change?
12. Understand work trends?
13. Follow up on career planning?
14. Follow up on promotion?
15. Follow up on career advancement and success?

Index